CRITICISM
AND TRUTH

THINKING LITERATURE
A series edited by Nan Z. Da and Anahid Nersessian

Criticism and Truth

ON METHOD IN LITERARY STUDIES

Jonathan Kramnick

The University of Chicago Press
Chicago and London

The University of Chicago Press, Chicago 60637
The University of Chicago Press, Ltd., London
© 2023 by The University of Chicago
All rights reserved. No part of this book may be used or reproduced
in any manner whatsoever without written permission, except
in the case of brief quotations in critical articles and reviews. For
more information, contact the University of Chicago Press, 1427
East 60th Street, Chicago, IL 60637.
Published 2023
Printed in the United States of America

32 31 30 29 28 27 26 25 24 23   1 2 3 4 5

ISBN-13: 978-0-226-83052-0 (cloth)
ISBN-13: 978-0-226-83053-7 (paper)
ISBN-13: 978-0-226-83054-4 (e-book)
DOI: https://doi.org/10.7208/chicago/9780226830544.001.0001

Library of Congress Cataloging-in-Publication Data

Names: Kramnick, Jonathan Brody, author.
Title: Criticism and truth : on method in literary studies / Jonathan
    Kramnick.
Other titles: Thinking literature.
Description: Chicago : The University of Chicago Press, 2023. |
    Series: Thinking literature | Includes bibliographical references
    and index.
Identifiers: LCCN 2023014969 | ISBN 9780226830520 (cloth)
    | ISBN 9780226830537 (paperback) | ISBN 9780226830544
    (ebook)
Subjects: LCSH: Criticism.
Classification: LCC PN81 .K6958 2023 | DDC 801/.95—dc23/
    eng/20230612
LC record available at https://lccn.loc.gov/2023014969

♾ This paper meets the requirements of ANSI/NISO Z39.48-1992
(Permanence of Paper).

Contents

Preface

I wanted to give an account of literary studies as an academic discipline. I didn't want to write a historical study, however, or to claim that our present situation is best analyzed in comparison with an older one. Excellent books of this kind already exist, and I thought a certain clarity and precision might be gained by taking a snapshot of work in the field. I wanted to focus on the distinctive methodology of literary criticism and describe how the practice finds a grip on the world. My reasons were simple, although they had taken on more urgency during the writing. I had for some time been working to understand criticism within a broader picture of the disciplines. Every discipline of study contributes in its own way to making the world intelligible, I had argued, and none ought to be reduced to another. But I hadn't yet looked closely enough at actual instances of criticism with a view to their status as method. The time had come, I thought, to consider the positive contributions of the field in its granular particularity. In the event, my goal was neither to advocate for something old nor urge that we create something new. It was instead to present a view of literary criticism as it is practiced across the academy in order to defend its standing as a contribution to knowledge.

Celebrating what we do strikes me as unusual and timely. For all the varied defenses of the humanities out there, and for all the attention to the history and current state of literary studies, there have been, of late, few positive characterizations of literary critical method. Recent events have made it urgent to fill that void. When I began writing in defense of disciplinary thinking, every humanities field had for some time been subject to conditions of austerity. Nothing, however, could prepare us for the emergency that followed. The decimation of higher education during the COVID-19 era would all but eliminate jobs for younger scholars, threatening intellectual continuity from one generation to the next, and so put in peril the very existence of the discipline itself. Much now remains unclear, but the urgent task for those of us who write from relative security is to make this situation better. In this context, it seems to me that we don't need one person's single-minded program for how literary criticism ought to change. We need a defense of work that is already being done and an account of why it should flourish.

For the same reason, it seems to me that we don't need a long book. I have not attempted to be comprehensive. I have attempted rather to isolate and explain some common and foundational practices that (along with others) might be said to ground literary studies as a discipline of knowledge. I have attempted as well to give an original account of these practices, drawing on my interest in ecological modes of thinking, skilled engagement with the world, and craft as a way of knowing. To go on for too long like this would surely personalize the argument in ways that undercut its validity. The urgency of the moment calls for something brief and sharp and portable.

Jonathan Kramnick
Hamden, CT

Craft Knowledge [INTRODUCTION]

If I must ascribe a meaning to the word craftsmanship, I shall say as a first approx-
imation that it means simply workmanship using any kind technique or apparatus,
in which the quality of the result is not predetermined, but depends on the judgment,
dexterity and care which the maker exercises as he works. The essential idea is that
the quality of the result is continually at risk during the process of making; and so I
shall call this kind of workmanship "The workmanship of risk": an uncouth phrase,
but at least descriptive.

DAVID PYE, *The Nature and Art of Workmanship* (1968)

This is a short book making a case for literary studies as a discipline
of study. Every discipline has one or more methods that ground its
authority to tell truths about whatever part of the world it endeavors
to explain. *Criticism and Truth* examines the truth claims of literary
criticism by focusing on close reading: a baseline practice and proprietary method for pursuing arguments and advancing knowledge
in the field. I analyze what makes literary studies like and unlike
other disciplines, not only in the rest of the humanities but in the social and natural sciences as well. My goal is to spend some time with
the methods particular to literary studies and so provide a concise
account of its distinctive epistemology considered as one part of a
multidisciplinary and pluralist university. My goal, in other words,
is to advocate for humanistic expertise as something equivalent to
the expertise of the sciences and for literary criticism as an activity
undertaken by one discipline among an array of disciplines.

I am writing this book at a moment of intense worry about the future of the humanities and intense reconsideration of what critics
do and how we do it. In broad form, such concerns are of course not
new. For some time, the discipline of literary studies in particular

has understood itself to be in decline relative both to its former stature and to what we now call the STEM disciplines. What John Guillory described as a loss of cultural capital has left the discipline especially vulnerable to the defunding and austerity visited in general upon universities over the past several decades.[1] But all of this has accelerated, and the institutional worries are now existential. The present moment stands out in review. When the pandemic hit university finances in 2020, humanities disciplines were already in the throes of a decade-long crisis in employment, with the number of tenure-track jobs diminishing every year and a transition to adjunct or otherwise precarious labor well under way.[2] The COVID-related hiring freezes and layoffs made all of that worse, exacerbating inequalities among strata of the academic workforce and diminishing prospects for a generation of younger scholars. The ultimate consequences of the employment crisis will not be clear for some time. What it has brought to the surface, however, is that no discipline of study is separate from its material conditions: jobs, classrooms, libraries, laboratories, and an infrastructure of training from one generation to the next. Our worries are existential because we have had to contemplate the end to all of this, an extinction event in the history of knowledge, now fast, now slow, here visible, there hidden.

The collapse of the discipline risks many things, foremost among them the livelihood of younger scholars. The ethical and epistemic fallout here cannot be overstated. The first is perhaps clear enough to picture, even as it requires the constant attention of those like me whose careers have depended on life's toss of the generational dice. We owe it to those who have chosen our field to fight for its future and to use all the resources we have in the battle. The epistemic fallout, however, is inseparable and equally vital to imagine. In our agonizing about the jobs crisis, we sometimes bracket off talk about employment from talk about the rest of what happens in the discipline, but hiring cuts across and sustains all of academic life. It is the very means by which any discipline survives and changes over time. Disciplines survive by hiring because new positions maintain the skills and knowledge base for ongoing teaching and research. Younger scholars moving up through the ranks develop, refine, and renew the living practice of the field. For this reason, they provide the very impetus for all scholarly engagement. To whom is one writing if not the scholars of the future? Everyone participates in this process, whether they are faculty in graduate programs or not. Every time we write, we are engaging topics, pursuing methods, and visiting archives in such a way that provides a model for others to follow. We are asking questions that will be answered by those who come after us, using tools they have learned from us. At the same time, younger scholars challenge how these questions have been asked, sharpen the tools used to answer them, and create altogether new paths of inquiry. Senior scholars cannot be trusted to challenge their own assumptions about what counts as a good reading or a solid argument, about whose perspectives and what archives ought to be consulted, about what questions are vital to ask and how to go about asking them. Hiring sustains the counterflow of ideas and practices from the young to the old. It makes sure that academic discussions don't calcify into a liturgy or disappear altogether.

The collapse of the discipline risks our knowing less about the world, about works of literature and the people who create and read them. That is to put the loss rather simply and starkly, but also to focus our attention on the epistemic rationale for what we do. The practice of teaching and writing in a discipline is, in one way or another, the practice of creating and disseminating knowledge.

So much should go without saying, and yet needs to be said all the time. Like any other discipline, the study of literature is the *study of* a part of the world that is presumed to be important for collective flourishing. Every discipline of study makes a claim for its own existence along these lines, whether its domain is numbers or networks or novels. Academic work contributes to making the world intelligible and so transforming it for the better. The study of literature is one part of that project, and its practice is the creation of knowledge worth having. Once again, however, this practice doesn't exist on its own. It is grounded in syllabi, in methods of argument, in archives that compel inquiry, topics that inspire debate, and above all in the very human labor presently under considerable duress. Much of the recent meta-discussion of method in the literary disciplines has proceeded at a remove from these conditions. By contrast, this book keeps in mind the present situation of literary studies within the university and the university within the world. Along the same lines, it locates method in actual practice rather than in ideas about practice. I dig into elemental features of critical writing in order to defend their epistemology. Now in the moment of austerity might be a good time to do this.

The ethos of *Criticism and Truth* is democratic and disinterested. I don't have a new method of reading to advertise, and I don't want to tell critics to stop doing one thing in order to do something else. Rather, I want to provide an account of what we already do so as to advocate for its good standing. The book is a defense of the everyday science and ordinary expertise of work in literary studies as it happens all the time and everywhere, in published criticism and the classroom. Anyone who reads or writes academic books or articles in English or in comparative literature or in one of the foreign language disciplines is intimately familiar with this everyday science and ordinary expertise. Take a look at your own work or the work of a colleague; pull a book off your shelf or download a recent issue of a journal. Examine how the sentences treat their objects of inquiry, how the argument proceeds within the shape of a sentence and from one sentence to the next. What you see is a carefully considered practice of expertise, something developed and perfected over time in the life of a critic. No one comes by this practice easily. It is a skill learned by training and sharpened by imitation, failure, correction, and improvement. I want to give an account of this skill in the act of writing criticism and to defend its relation to knowledge.

I will have much to say about the epistemology of skill in subsequent chapters and will argue that *knowing how* to write about texts in a certain way is an important means of *knowing that* something is so with them and their worlds of composition and reference. To help me with this argument, I make use from time to time of works written in the discipline of academic philosophy, particularly works of epistemology (naturally enough) as well as the philosophy of science. In keeping with my defense of the standing of literary studies, however, I am more interested in thinking with the philosophy than ceding ground to that discipline on matters of truth and method. Philosophy just happens to provide a source of ideas and discussion about actions, knowledge, and skilled engagement with the world. But so do some of the more self-conscious reflections of literary critics, and both have helped me make sense of the immersive practice of writing we call close reading.

For the purposes of introducing the topic, therefore, allow me to begin even further afield with the anthropologist Tim Ingold discussing the skilled practice of weaving bags among the Telefol people of Papua New Guinea. No one is born with this particular competence. It is acquired by means of careful instruction and acculturation. Brought into the practice, the novice learns to feel strings of equal weight and length, draw them to tightness between the fingers and thigh, and carry each through a sustained looping motion from front to back. Over time and through "repeated practical trials, and guided by his observations," the novice "learns to fine-tune his own movements so as to achieve the rhythmic fluency of the accomplished practitioner." This is a process of situated attunement, in which the weaver moves her hands and holds herself in such a way that gets a handle on some piece of the world in order to make it into something else. Skilled practice of this kind "is not just the application of mechanical force to exterior objects," Ingold reflects, "but entails qualities of care, judgment, and dexterity.... Whatever practitioners do *to* things is grounded in an attentive, perceptual involvement *with* them."[3] Importantly for my current purposes, to know how to get the weave right is to know something about the properties of string, the tensile strength of loops and knots, and the shape and movement of bodies, artifacts, and cultures. In this respect, skilled practice is a special case of craft knowledge. One learns something about the world through a physical and creative encounter with it. The process is physical because it involves a whole body reaching out to pieces of an environment that already have a certain heft or structure. It is creative because something is made from that environment, which is then altered and adjusted in turn. "Learning is inseparable from doing," each "embedded in the context of practical engagement with the world" (416). The weaver doesn't apply an already-formed idea to string, like a signet on wax. Rather, the movement of her fingers "carries its own intentionality, quite apart from any designs or plans that it may be supposed to implement." When a bag takes shape from fibers, "it is the activity itself—of regular, controlled movement— that generates the form, not the design that precedes it" (354). To practice a craft is in this way to know something about the world as you are situated in it and make something from it, all at once and at the same time.

I begin with an example from the anthropology of skill precisely because it appears so far away from writing sentences of criticism. My epigraph from David Pye's classic study of craft aesthetics serves a similar point. Craftwork requires the "judgment, care, and dexterity" of someone whose understanding of the world at hand guides a result that is always at risk. The radical dislocation in each case might draw out features of skill in our craft of composing sentences from sentences, working with materials that limit and shape what we may do with them, and thus learning and transmitting something about their specific nature. This book will return in several guises to the central idea that our method lies in a hands-on relation to our objects and our creating something from them. Close reading is a craft because it is a skilled practice of making sentences from sentences that are already in the world, the immersive environment of the literary. One learns how to do this. Close reading is also a craft because it is a method of understanding that environment. One lesson from the anthropology of skill, of real significance for the epistemic and disciplinary issues I discuss in subsequent chapters, is that knowledge of the world cannot be separated from interaction with the world. When Ingold asserts that "skill is the foundation from which all knowledge flows," he means to disclose the know-how of fingers grasping on to and manipulating fiber. He also means that deft movement of this kind tells you something about what is grasped and what is made and their worlds of significance.[4]

But the materials one works with set limits to what may be done with them. That is what it means to grasp on to something that is already there, with a certain composition and a certain structure. Another lesson from the anthropology of skill, therefore, is that the world pushes back. To practice a craft is to create within the constraints of what is given. One gets things right with skilled attunement, and one gets things wrong when skill falters and doesn't hit the mark. This, too, will be important to remember. We learn about the world through skilled engagement with its particular nature, but we also make mistakes or errors. Not every performance is what the philosopher Ernest Sosa calls an "apt performance," and not all work is good work.[5]

Mistake and revision are integral to the production and dissemination of knowledge no matter what the field. They are held in check by the processes of validation we call peer review and evaluation, the means for establishing consensus as well as dissensus in the appraisal of truth claims. Skill also doesn't exist on its own. A performance is apt when it is recognized as so, when it is confirmed as adroit, perspicuous, and elegant by those equipped to judge. I'll have more to say about how this works with respect to writing in the field. The important point now is just to register that such writing has a discipline-specific method of getting a handle on the literary by working with and creating something from its form. I have written elsewhere in defense of an elastic meaning of the term "form" for criticism, a matter of some debate over the past decade or so.[6] I intend here just to point to the irreducibly linguistic nature of our objects of study and to the important fact that we engage, brush up against, and interpret these objects in the same linguistic medium. To get a handle on the literary is to attune one's own words to the words of another. Those words set limits to what one can do with them.

At the same time, the kinds of questions one might ask or the inquiries one might engage in have no limits at all. This is an important point to stress when we consider close reading as a method, located in a discipline of study. For some, the idea that close reading is a proprietary method of the literary humanities might seem restrictive and exclusionary, to block, for example, work that is more historical or political in its aims and topics. I want to clarify at the outset that this is not how I see things. The deft treatment of language—the craftwork of spinning sentences from sentences already in the world—is just a discipline-specific way that the literary humanities tell important truths about the world. This holds across the many topics, traditions, ways of life and feeling that preoccupy literary studies today and the infinite number that might tomorrow. My point is only that we can get a better handle on the heterogeneous work being done in the field, and advocate for its place in a multidisciplinary university, if we can form a picture of the skill that goes into treating our objects of inquiry and recognize the knowledge that would be lost with its passing.

The example from anthropology serves in this last respect one further use. Philosophy and criticism do not have well-developed ideas of extinction. The term is more familiar to the science that tracks the survival of human life-forms and their methods of interacting with and knowing the world. Ways of living die. Nothing in what we do survives without care. Recent years have made all too clear that the human labor of writing and teaching is the lifeblood of the discipline. The human labor of writing and teaching creates knowledge as well as sustains the practice as a model to learn and transform over time. None of this subsists on its own. Each requires support and sustenance from the institutions in which disciplines live. We are in a time of radical habitat destruction.

*   *   *

Everyone in a discipline employs highly rarefied skills peculiar to their field of study, whether that is work in a lab or an archive or with texts. The craftwork methods of a discipline aren't capacities one is born with like binocular vision. They are learned practices of creating knowledge. Skill is in this way an exclusive kind of thing, something one has that others don't. At the same time, skill is something everyone within a given discipline has. I want to underscore that ubiquity as part of the democratic ethos of this book, its celebration of the work done everywhere, all the time. I also want to underscore that skill has an epistemic function and is fundamental to method. Skills pick out features of the world, and do so by means of the unique way they are situated within disciplines. Close reading is different from concomitant variation, which is different from regression analyses. I want to draw attention finally to the fragility of all this. Every method of every discipline tells us something about some unique corner of the world. Every method and the truths they disclose might be lost.

It is easy to overlook the highly skilled practices that ground a discipline of knowledge. After a time, many become so intuitive that they pass unnoticed. *Criticism and Truth* aims to make some of that intuitive knowledge explicit by looking at the virtuosity of everyday practice in the field, drawing it out in the open, and providing an account of how it tells truths about texts and worlds. Much of the recent discussion of method in literary studies hasn't really been about method at all, but rather an occasion for a proxy debate about what sort of attitude one should bear to their objects of study and, beneath that, a proxy debate about whether and to what extent it is important to claim relevance for interpretive work at a moment of crisis for the discipline's footing in the academy and the academy's footing in the world. I take no stand in these debates, except to say that no discipline can be relevant without having a secure lock on knowledge, and that no discipline *is* relevant if it ceases to exist. My response to the method debates, therefore, is to shift the terrain to actual practice and so to the way truth claims are advanced in literary studies—in other words, to introduce the topic of method qua method. In order to do this, I focus on procedures of critical writing designed to brush up against and make something from the immersive environment of the literary: the writing of criticism as a kind of craft and the epistemology of close reading as a kind of craft knowledge.

One of the most immersive and engaged practices of writing is quotation. There is no more direct way to reach out to and make something from a linguistic artifact than to wrap your words around it, to accommodate your syntax to syntax already arranged by mood, number, and tense. I therefore begin with and return frequently to the micro-procedures of quotation in works of criticism. I am interested in how critics embed language within and between their sentences, as part of the unit they are composing or as independent blocks adjacent to their prose. Quotation is in this way an important instance of a broader practice of adjusting one's language to language that constrains and enables what one may do with it. But there are others, from unmarked procedures of *sounding like* the text one is writing about, or what we might call critical free indirect discourse, to story-building acts of interpretive plot summary and beyond. Practices like these require a great deal of often tacit know-how, and, in the act, they tell us something important about the encountered world. They are not the whole of close reading or of method in the literary humanities. I make no such immodest claim. They are, however, an essential part of both: a means to get a handle on our objects of interest by getting them right.

The book moves through a discussion of close reading as method, method as skilled practice, practice as creative action, and creative action as justified truth. I investigate the way that the most everyday acts of writing shape novel objects in the act of having something to say about them. I argue that critical practice is creative in this way because it makes something new and something valuable, and that judgment of critical works by peers is among other things an evaluation of how well that making is done. I do not argue, however, that the creative dimension of critical writing is simply balanced by its epistemic dimension. Looking at a range of examples from the long contemporary period, I argue instead that the two are inseparable, that criticism is true when it is apt, false when it is formed poorly. If the collective appraisal of critical writing is for this reason something of an aesthetic judgment, it is one that examines how carefully the writing has worked with its materials. I will therefore spend some time establishing how the recognition of skill and artistry forms one basis among others for the collective appraisal and verification of individual works of criticism. Judgment of this sort concerns the compelling treatment of some part of the world, whose particular nature sets limits for what may be made from it. In this way, to recognize creativity in criticism is to deepen rather than move away from an emphasis on method as an instrument of truth because it is to draw attention to the fine structure of unique artifacts: criticism's new sentences woven from old. It is to draw attention to how some sentences stay true to others by embedding or extending them well.

The craft of composing these sentences means that an important part of their knowledge work lies in the doing, in the apt placement of words up against or amid words already there, not in thoughts or ideas or even research that precede the act itself. I want to point to the *action* of criticism as part of a larger commitment to the idea that knowledge and perception are embodied and environmentally situated rather than contemplative or detached phenomena.[7] We perceive and know through the fingers. In the present context, this is to emphasize the practical dimension of critical practice, the actual procedures that make method methodical and fasten words to the world. I put practice in the foreground because I'm interested in how criticism is done. I am aiming to ground our talk about method in method while also grounding method in an academic system transformed by 2008 and then again by 2020. One important feature of this period is the effort to imagine that criticism might have an audience or even a home outside the university. I close therefore with a consideration of scholarly method outside its conventional location and ask what happens to the procedures of interpretation and explanation when they aren't directed at other practitioners of the craft, by means of the usual, restricted routes of communication, but rather at the public itself as part of a public humanities. This is an important question to consider because it gets to the heart of disciplinary survival and extinction. I'll ask whether and to what extent a public humanities can sustain and enliven methods of inquiry when there may be no feedback (or -forward) from the audience itself and when the practice occurs largely without an infrastructure of employment. The public humanities are evidently critical for the survival of the field and important to cultivate and describe, as I will attempt to do. They are also part of a larger ecology that we ought to understand in the details. This book does not attempt anything like a comprehensive picture of that ecology, just a meaningful slice through a vital part of it.

Method Talk

Does literary criticism tell truths about the world? This is a question scholars of literature don't often ask, or don't often ask directly, but it gets to the heart of how work in the discipline is done and why the discipline exists in the first place. One way to answer the question is to examine whether criticism attempts to make true statements about literary texts and, if so, by what means its statements are judged as true or false. How do we encounter and interact with our objects of study? Where does our writing begin and the writing we're writing about end? How are consensus judgments about the validity or perspicuity or elegance of a reading made? Another way to come at this question is to examine whether criticism is capable in some fashion of telling truths about the world itself, not just the small piece of it called literature. Does criticism about ecology or consciousness, to take examples from my own work (and feel free to insert your own), tell some truth about ecology or consciousness themselves? I think we'd all like to believe that it does, but how? Both lines of inquiry take aim at method and therefore at epistemology. They ask how critical practice—writing about writing— purports to convey knowledge, whether that is knowledge about literature or knowledge about the world in which literature is one part. This book is an effort to consider these two sides of the relation between criticism and truth.

We need to talk about method. That might seem like a strange thing to say, considering that until recently literary study was caught up in what some called "the method wars."[1] The term was coined by Rita Felski to provide a name for debates between various types of reading and quarrels over the status of critique, where reading refers to practices of interpretation and critique to political scrutiny or judgment.[2] I don't intend to add to these debates. As the expression goes, they seem already to have run out of steam. I bring up this recent episode in the history of the discipline rather because of a curiously unfulfilled promise in its stated itinerary. Felski claimed that the debates she was interested in were about "the various procedures and practices that inform our encounter with a text," but on inspection their actual content always seemed to be about something else.[3] Just when we might have expected a discussion of argument and evidence in literary studies, the topic turned instead, in Felski and Elizabeth Anker's words, to matters of "tone, attitude, or sensibility," to "ethos or affect," and especially to the variously affirming or paranoid, reparative or suspicious "moods" of criticism and critics alike.[4] Quarrels about method were, in other words, really quarrels about what critics believed was the appropriate stance to take toward literary texts and other objects of study, and especially whether one ought to put in the foreground the pleasure to be found in artworks or the politics beneath their creation, meaning, and circulation. The procedures in which arguments were made and the manner in which texts were treated remained the same across both sides of the divide, only the attitudes and bearings were different. It is for this reason hard not to agree with David Kurnick's assessment that "although it has become common to refer to this miniature tradition as about method," the critical texts at the center of these debates "offer not new ways to interpret texts but new ways to feel about ourselves when we do."[5] The method wars were about many things—the self-assessment and anxieties of a discipline unsure of its present importance or future existence, for example—but they weren't really about method, weren't really about our actual on-the-ground procedures of reading and interpretation.

That is a shame. Methods are distinct from the topics and feelings that accompany them, as fascinating and important as these topics and feelings might be. They describe points of attachment between a practice and the rest of the world and are designed to make that world intelligible. To think about method qua method, therefore, is to consider how we make arguments and how our procedures of truth telling stack up against those of disciplines with which we sometimes imagine ourselves in conversation. To think in this way is important because methods ground the authority of any discipline of study, whether those in the humanities or those in the social and natural sciences. Every one of them has a distinctive way of asking questions that it finds of interest. Every one of them has a distinctive way of presenting and evaluating evidence, of telling the truth in other words. There is, if one looks, a loose consensus when it comes to methods in our own discipline, I think, even as there is disagreement in our talk about method. We just haven't yet or haven't recently paused to look at them carefully. Method talk should include reflections on everyday practice. Now is a very good time to do some of this reflection, as the literary humanities' place among the array of disciplines seems increasingly insecure and as the academy as a whole finds itself subject to austerity and the amalgamation of its parts. Getting a better sense of our methods alone will not save literary studies. That will require a broader campaign to fund and rebuild universities. But defending the role of humanistic expertise in the explanation and transformation of the world is likely a necessary part of that campaign.

I am arguing that to understand the methods of literary study we should turn to practice. We should turn to the everyday activities that create and disseminate knowledge in the field and therefore secure its authority as an academic discipline. The philosopher Alasdair MacIntyre defines practice as a "coherent and complex form of socially established cooperative human activity through which goods internal to that form of activity are realized in the course of trying to achieve those standards of excellence which are appropriate to, and partially definitive of that form of activity."[6] This is a compressed and difficult formulation, but I think it is a helpful synopsis all the same. The practices of writing and teaching realize, among other goods, the epistemic goal of understanding and learning about the world. They do so according to standards of excellence at once widely held and subject to change. MacIntyre's compact account is just a nice way to see how this is all bundled together in forms of activity like leading discussions or composing sentences. Each follows "socially established" patterns and goals, and each is subject to standards that mark out the practice and its goods. None is done on its own. Actual work in a discipline requires one to recognize how much others know and one doesn't, a loss in ego that brings a gain in skill. "To enter into a practice is to accept the authority of those standards and the inadequacy of my own performance in relation to them. It is to submit my own attitudes, choices, preferences and tastes to the standards which currently and partially define the practice" (190). MacIntyre describes here the experience of acculturation into a craft, but also a subordination to external measure that lasts as long as one is active.

One is always subject to another's judgment, and one is always honing one's craft. This "subordinating ourselves within the practice to other practitioners" describes the structure of validation in the field, the appraisal of work as apt, well-formed, and true (191). At the same time, the addition of the adverbs "currently and partially" is important because it recognizes that work in a practice modifies a practice over time. "Standards are not themselves immune to criticism," but rather something made and remade as they are inhabited (190).

Academic practices are living phenomena. They have no existence apart from the work of those who are brought into them, and, like anything alive, they require care to avoid deterioration or death. The care they require, however, is not simply being taken up and passed on; it is also being transformed by those who want to do things differently from what they have been taught. No living craft remains always the same, for the reason that practitioners alter what they have learned, even slightly, in the effort to do work better or toward different ends. The current crisis in finding employment for younger scholars has reminded us of that all too well, as it has posed such sharp disruption to every discipline's pattern of challenging as well as sustaining the work of the field. The life of criticism requires real-world agents to renew as well as perform the craft.

Literary critics do lots of things in the course of their work: answer email, read and write, teach classes, attend meetings, order books. Only some of that activity is practice and thus central to method in the sense I will be using the term. Only some is involved with making intelligible its corner of the world. My interests in this book are with inquiry as it is happening. I want to look at method in action, at critics reaching out to and creating something from other people's sentences, turning their objects of analysis, and compelling assent as careful and judicious while they do so.

In making the claim that method lies in practice rather than ideas about practice, my argument is in keeping with Rachel Sagner Buurma and Laura Heffernan's recent attempt to reorient collective discussion in the field to the everyday life of the classroom. Manifestos "dominate our metadiscourse while misrepresenting our practice," Buurma and Heffernan argue, because the abstraction and remove of the genre tends to exaggerate disagreement. In contrast, a focus on the ordinary procedures and routines of the discipline "reveals interconnections rather than oppositions and continuities rather than ruptures."[7] Pause to look at what critics actually do—the "practitioners' own experience"—and you'll see that we actually do something similar, even at radically different locations and with respect to widely divergent subject matter (7). Buurma and Heffernan's turn to practice, however, points to a different area of activity from what I have been and will be discussing. "The true history of English literary study resides in classrooms," they argue. "In classrooms, teachers and students have invented and perfected the core methods of literary study" (3). Therefore "classrooms offer us both a truer and more usable account of what literary study is and does" than accounts that focus on the monograph or polemic (6). Like Buurma and Heffernan, I think that the meaningful ground of the discipline lies in its everyday practice, but I do not see that practice residing in the classroom more than in written scholarship. Rather, the two form an indissoluble whole. As magical and essential as the classroom is, the written, published, and circulated form of criticism is indispensable for the constitution of the field as a field. At a minimum, it secures what Eric Havelock, describing Plato's writing down of Socratic dialogue, calls "storage for re-use," so that knowledge extends from the single location of a given class to the community of critics at large and from the eighty or so minutes of a seminar to the durée of an article or book.[8] As with equivalent forms for other disciplines, such as the peer-reviewed study or the proof or the program, written and published criticism allows scholars to engage with, extend, and revise the arguments of nonpresent others as they situate themselves with respect to works and worlds they intend to understand. The peculiar rules of written criticism cannot for this reason be bypassed or dissolved into pedagogy. They are integral to anyone's orientation to the field and the field's orientation to the world.

Focusing on scholarship doesn't mean, however, that one puts the priority on metadiscourse or elite publications or famous critics at wealthy universities. Like the practice of teaching classes, the practice of writing criticism is a baseline activity of the field. Everyone writes. At some point, everyone publishes. My question is what do literary critics actually do when they write about texts? The answer, as I will explore in the next chapter, contains a further argument. When Buurma and Heffernan claim that "more poems have been close-read in classrooms than in published articles," they identify the coruscating zigzag of seminar discussion with the sculpted form of the argumentative sentence (2). And yet the relation between the two is neither necessary nor direct. One writes and publishes about material one doesn't teach, and one teaches material one doesn't write about, all the time. When the journey from classroom discussion to published criticism happens, as it sometimes does, it can seem miraculous and is to be valued immensely. But even then, an important series of changes occurs. Halting and interrupted expressions of excitement fall away or remain standing; digressions smooth into lines; and, most importantly, words once spoken in a student's or instructor's voice wrap themselves around and fasten themselves to words in a stranger's idiom. All of that takes work, and all of that creates something new: a series of connected sentences that then circulates as the final product to be read, referred to, and quarreled with. This is the argument introduced in answer to my question: What do literary critics actually do when they write about texts? Close reading isn't reading. It's writing. The practice we usually refer to when we talk about method is finally a written one.

In subsequent chapters, I will examine the craft of joining one's words to words that already have order and form. I would just observe now that this work is different in kind from the craft of teaching and that neither one sits below the other at the foundation of the discipline. Buurma and Heffernan are right, I think, that method wars are sprinkled at the edges of the profession while method itself is everywhere and in common practice. They are also right that common practice has a common shape. Drill down to craftwork in action, and you will see a loose consensus concerning what to do and how to do it. That might seem like a strange claim to make at first blush, since our field, like every other one, is marked by debate, often of a most rancorous sort. Even as scholarly disagreement in our field happens all the time, however, it occurs less in the procedures in which readings gel than in the conclusions that readings draw and the lessons that readings proffer, with sometimes the stated or implied claim that a critic's failure to perform the craft well has led to the objectionable result. How a field of knowledge includes tacit consensus over method alongside structured dissensus over what method reveals is a fascinating topic in the epistemology of disagreement, as I will discuss later. The point here is simply that method is practice, practice is common, and common practice is epistemic.

The turn to practice is an attempt to understand what grounds the authority of the discipline considered among an array of disciplines. Looking at pedagogy is one way to do so, and looking at scholarship another. For some in literary studies, by way of contrast, the best way to ground the authority of the discipline is to look *elsewhere* for methods that might have more quantitative heft, to look at computer science or statistics, for example. This effort to look elsewhere for method often contains the accompanying claim that literary studies has no method, or at least not one that has epistemic standing. The argument sets the discipline, as it were, against itself. Andrew Piper, for example, has argued that what passes for method in criticism is nothing short of an "epistemological tragedy" because it fails to generalize beyond or even really within the singular case of a particular text.[9] In its ordinary form, he says, criticism cannot move from its limited set of words or lines or blocks to any larger unit, whether the literary work or its historical situation, without an unwarranted leap of inference. This is the "crisis … at the core of literary criticism, an incommensurable relation between part and whole"; any artifact of culture is always a "flawed portal to understanding something larger than itself" (7). Close reading of the sort done by the many may be elegant at the level of the sentence, therefore, but actual knowledge requires a prosthesis done by the few. It is "computational literary criticism" that "sets as its task a reflection on the representativeness of its own evidence" and so provides a "science of generalization" (8–9).

Method on this view is something other disciplines have, and knowledge is something other disciplines create. The claim identifies a classical problem in interpretation—the movement from part to whole, individual text to larger genre, literature to culture and history—and decides it is fatally unsolvable, at least on its own.[10]

There is of course no shortage of discussion of this interpretive problem in the history of criticism and theory, from well before the discipline emerged to, one imagines, well after it ends. The computational argument against business as usual is worth our attention, however, because it helps to clarify by way of its estrangement from everyday practice precisely what actual everyday method in the business is and who actually is doing it. Two of the argument's maneuvers are important in this regard. The first is the demotion of craftwork to charisma. The long, elaborate moment when the medium of criticism brushes up against the medium of literature, when words weave with words, is the occasion for a critic's impressions, not a practice that bears and creates knowledge. The second is the paralysis of scale. Not only is writing at the micro-level without epistemic significance, but the effort to build from the fine grain is unearned conjecture. A valid movement of scale requires the application of technology, of the sort that might churn "3,338,230 punctuation marks ... 1.4 billion words ... or 650,000 fictional characters" (3). Understood in this fashion, knowledge in the literary disciplines attaches only to the surrogated method of the sciences with their norms of openness and publicness and their practices of replication.[11]

One virtue of this argument for my current purposes is that it might be flipped over to show what method in the literary humanities looks like. I'll discuss in later chapters some of the ways in which methods and norms suited to the sciences, including especially those of replication, don't suit the humanities. You can't repeat someone else's reading, nor should you try to. Nor is that something to lament. To do so would be to confuse method in the sciences for method as such. The ill-fitting demand for something like replication reveals, however, a humanistic practice that works well in a very different way. The micro-procedures of literary analysis, for example, are skilled actions. One can't do them without training. Over time, one becomes equipped with the knowledge to perform the action in a way that is adept and that seems on reflection, especially by others, to half create, half pick out features of the world that are true. The skilled practice of writing criticism discloses in this respect two related but distinct kinds of knowledge. One knows how to do something, and then one knows something to be the case (about, for example, a text or its culture). What relation holds between these two forms of knowledge? And how does a reading at the micro-level of words and sentences scale up to one at the macro-level of works, genres, and cultures? These are hard questions, but they are not in principle impossible to answer. They touch the epistemic foundation of the discipline. We can catch a glimpse of this foundation when we compare it with that of disciplines whose practices are different from ours. Replication fits a practice designed to seem from nowhere and to be available from all points of view, but not one that fastens one view to another, language that belongs to one person to language that belongs to someone else.

I don't mean to gripe against computational forms of criticism as such, just their occasional claim to occupy the epistemic high ground. It surely can't be the case that only a tiny, well-funded part of the discipline traffics in truth while the rest is mired in error. (If it is, we need far more than machines to save us.) Such claim making is, in any case, as unnecessary as it is unwarranted. Computational criticism construes its objects at a different magnitude from the conventional practices of literary interpretation, but that doesn't give it a more compelling purchase on truth. It just shows how truth—perspicuity, elegance, and dexterity in an explanatory context—corresponds to method. This is to weigh the relative contributions of close reading and computational analysis on the terms suggested by the epistemologist Simon Blackburn in his recent monograph *On Truth*. "Instead of facts first, with method analyzed in terms of its contribution to fact," Blackburn writes, "we look at the methods first, and then describe fact in terms of the ideal endpoint (which we may never reach) of satisfactory applications of method. The question at the forefront of our minds should not be 'what is aesthetic (etc.) fact?' but 'what makes for a good aesthetic (etc.) inquiry?'"[12] All methods on this view apply skilled practices to their particular corners of the world. These practices just vary according to the specific nature of what is being studied. The "satisfactory application" of computational analysis and that of close reading will be different in the extreme, corresponding to objects of wholly different size. Viewed this way, computational criticism needn't be seen to correct the practice of almost everyone in the discipline. It merely stands athwart it, doing something else, either well or poorly according to criteria specific to the method. Likewise close reading. A pluralistic discipline should be able to contain both, and on occasion combine the two for a kind of interdisciplinarity within literary studies itself.[13] In the present context, the suspicion of business as usual is another good reason to look at our existing practices for unexpressed or overlooked coherence and thus get a sense of the method that already grounds the truth claims of everyday work in the discipline. To get a sense of these claims might be a good idea for the several reasons I have belabored: It might provide an account of the epistemic rationale of literary studies at a moment when some believe that the discipline has no such rationale; it might provide an account of interdisciplinarity that respects the validity and separate procedures of the disciplines from which it is made.[14] It might do all this as universities face unprecedented financial and political difficulty.

One begins with a question and then reaches out in steady and controlled fashion to whatever is the subject of one's inquiry. This much, at least, is the same for any discipline of study. Method stirs the graspable world so that it responds to one's curiosity, whatever that may be, following whatever practices are suited to the task. "All phenomena, from the commonest everyday event to the most abstract processes of modern physics," as Michael Friedman put it in a classic study of scientific understanding, "are equally in need of explanation—although it is impossible, of course, that they all be explained at once."[15] That impossibility is why we have separate fields of study. It also marks the point at which similarity of method breaks down. Beyond the rudimentary sense that every kind of inquiry attaches a practice to a corner of the world, there is no single method that applies to the whole of learning, nor even within any branch of learning.[16] The very manner of attachment depends on context, on what skills fasten where and to what end. The chemist, the economist, and the critic all find themselves immersed in a world they endeavor to understand, using inherited tools and novel schemes to make a go of things as best they can. All are in the game of truth, but the rules are different for each.

The lesson is simple. Methodological pluralism is the key to grasping a world itself plural in structure. The questions one asks and the manner one answers take shape from the peculiar nature of what one wants to understand, whether that is Etruscan pottery or the existence of exoplanets. The literary humanities ask questions largely about the dominion of written language and embodied performance, aspects of linguistic culture approached and grasped by means of language. That fact puts all sorts of interesting and enabling constraints on method, as the record of the discipline attests. I will argue in the next chapter that it helps to explain the unique place of close reading as a baseline competence and proprietary method for the discipline. For now, I will just emphasize that field-specific methods consist of skilled practices designed for separate objects of study and that any effort to reduce the methods of one discipline to those of another is bound to fail.

I argued earlier that no method stays forever the same because each lives in the activity of scholars over the whole of their careers. "Practices never have a goal or goals fixed for all time," as MacIntyre puts it; rather, "the goals themselves are transmuted by the history of the activity," so that over the very long haul, even baseline procedures can shift noticeably (193–94). At the same time, however, the tight relation between a method and its objects means that the practical activity of a field can remain quite steady. Methods are stable yet not inflexible, we might say. Even as they change, they are also restricted by the nature of what they churn. The same is not the case for the topics and questions that methods put in play. As anyone who has ever served on a hiring committee or as a reader for a journal will testify, topics and questions in literary studies have no restrictions at all. They seem rather to take on the concerns of the world in vividly shifting order: climate change; surveillance and policing; state formation; race before race; categories of aesthetic experience; law and personhood; Blackness and ontology; the public meaning of poetic genres; sound, image, and writing; animals and animality; empire, economies, and oceans; and happily onward beyond what is presently imaginable. With respect to subject matter, eclecticism and heterogeneity have long been the order of the day. I'm inclined to think this is a good thing, but that is a matter for another discussion. I'm interested here in the relation between practical method and topical focus. There is, I think, a close link between the constraints of the one and the openness of the other. The relative stability of method provides torque and spin to the evolving concerns of the discipline, sometimes fast, sometimes slow, here abstract, there concrete. The very proliferation of inquiry, in other words, testifies to the rigor of method, as a core manner of asking and answering questions creates knowledge about everything literature itself addresses. It is because our inquiry has sure footing that it may range widely. Method is the steady ground for a worldliness that has no limits at all.

Close Reading

[CHAPTER TWO]

I have no desire to change the methods of literary studies. I want only to understand them. I want to understand everyday practice in the field as it is done everywhere, all the time, so as to make a case for the field as a discipline of knowledge. Literary critics do many things in the creation and circulation of knowledge, but when it comes to their published work, the practice that sets the discipline apart from others is close reading. That is a descriptive statement with at least as yet no value judgment attached. Few if any in literary studies would dispute the root importance of close reading for their discipline. That is why revisionary movements in the field invariably take reading as their target, as the thing to do differently or in some cases the thing not to do at all. If you want to strike at the symbolic as well as beating heart of literary studies, you take a shot at close reading. And you do that because you want to abrade the tacit recognition that close reading forms a baseline competence for work in the field; you want to upset the idea that it allows critics to pursue an infinite number of topics and make an infinite number of arguments. Any attempt to understand the methods particular to literary studies really ought to begin here.

In one way or another, everyone professes or is in flight from close reading. And yet what exactly is it? Ask any critic and they're likely to be brought up short. The question turns out to be very hard to answer. Unlike regression analysis or Bayesian inference, close reading just doesn't afford general characterization. The method is too sticky with respect to its materials to allow much in the way of abstraction across individual examples. This is not a scandal. In fact, I'm going to argue that the particularism of the method—its dwelling in instances of practice rather than formulas or guidelines for practice—ensures its good standing. To get something right about a sentence or set of sentences, one needs to make contact with and on many occasions incorporate their words and idiom. Doing so requires an adjustment to these words and idioms and sometimes a slight mimicry of them as well. The practice of writing about writing that results from this adjustment is just too various for a comprehensive definition of how it works as a method to seem anything other than inadequate or hubristic. For this reason, I will not attempt to give such a definition. I will instead keep the analysis to a size on which one might get traction. I will focus on several procedures involved in making contact with and incorporating objects of study in the analysis of them. Although these procedures are not the whole of close reading or of method, they are indispensable parts of each, with a good deal to reveal about the authority of the field.

Foremost among them are practices of quotation, whether embedding language from a text within your sentences, setting off larger gobbets in block form, or silently matching a text's tone and idiom through a kind of critical free indirect discourse. Quotation is important and revealing because it establishes a relation of skill between the critic and text. As I will attempt to show, embedding,

pointing to, and writing in the style of another's language are practiced means of attuning one's language to language that precedes
and limits one's writing. One learns how to do this continually with
every effort. At the same time, one learns *from* doing this about the
immersive environment of the literary. These practices are indispensable to the knowledge that circulates in public form as literary critical writing. There are, of course, other skills involved in the
work of the discipline. What makes quotation unique is its medium.
Or to make a finer point, what makes practices of quotation and its
near kin, free indirect discourse, unique is that they occur in the
same linguistic medium as their objects of study. They are an immersion at the microscale in the very stuff of literature. Few other
interpretive practices or methods of study are like that at all.

In the event, much of literary criticism turns on the art of quoting
well: pointing to lines or words of interest to your argument; placing new words up against or around them; describing how quoted
words sit among words unquoted or in the tradition of scholarly discussion. In this way, quotation is the art of moving across two orders
of writing, one's own and someone else's. One composes sentences
about and with sentences already made. In this space of maximal
proximity, quotation reveals something about close reading that we
have often gotten wrong. The expression "close reading" appears
to imply a particularly intense version of the ordinary practice of
reading, an especially hard concentration on the written word. As
an explanatory method, however, close reading is not exactly reading in that sense.[1] (As a classroom practice, it isn't either.)[2] It is not
a species of the mind's rapid decoding of the arbitrary symbols that
compose a language, what the neuroscientist Stanislas Dehaene
describes when he tracks "a printed word as it progresses from
the retina through a chain of processing stages, each of which is

marked by an elementary question: Are these letters? What do they look like? Are they a word? What does it sound like? How is it pronounced? What does it mean?"[3] Close reading requires all that to happen, but only to the extent that one must read as one writes. The interpretive work we call close reading rather is "*a genre of commentary*," in Andrew Goldstone's words, in which a critic writes about writing in order to pursue an idea or make a point or shed light on a topic.[4] Whether in scholarship or the classroom, commentary of this kind demands thought to be externalized in graphic or spoken form. It demands the active confrontation and commingling of one's own words and words out there in the world.

Such writing about writing is reading only in the metaphorical sense. Even so, we often lean hard on this metaphor when describing the work we do. "In the most common and least technical formulation," John Guillory maintains in a 2010 ADE (Association of Departments of English) forum on the topic, "close reading means paying attention to the words on the page."[5] In the same forum, Jonathan Culler defines the "practice of close reading" as "examining closely the language of a literary work."[6] More recently, Barbara Herrnstein Smith identifies the practice as "reading individual texts with attention to their linguistic features and rhetorical operations."[7] Also recently, and as a contribution to debates supposed to be about method, Toril Moi writes that "whether I do a postcolonial or a feminist or a psychoanalytic reading, methodologically I do the same sort of thing: I read. And to read is to pay attention to the particular text, to look and think in response to particular questions."[8] In another contribution to method talk, Heather Love adds that "the term *close reading* attempts to capture [a] reduction of scale, persistence, and temporally extended attention to the very small, and it is a hallmark of literary studies."[9] Varied as these and similar accounts are, each assumes close reading to be a type of reading. Each further assumes that an ideal of attentiveness distinguishes close reading from other kinds of reading: a "style of focus," in Natalie Phillips's terms, performed slowly in thoughtful rumination. Both assumptions are mistaken.[10]

The accounts I have just quoted share my hesitancy to define what close reading is. None is striving for any particular originality. The idea rather is to say something original only after passing through a minimal description of close reading as an especially attentive kind of reading. I want to take issue with the minimal description, however. When we model close reading as a type of reading, we remain within a visual and contemplative framework, understanding it to happen when eyes fix on words and then transmit a code to a thinking mind. "I look and think." This model of laborious, visual concentration is clearly seductive, both solemn and scholarly at once, but it loses the dimension of the practice better understood as craft. It loses how close reading is an expert practice of writing prose and making text, of weaving one's own words with words that precede and shape them. The loss is not small. As Elaine Auyoung has argued, "Our reliance on reading as a catchall term downplays the specialized nature of our critical practices." It is not (or not simply) the case that critics read slowly or with attention. "When we refer to what literary critics do as reading," Auyoung continues, "we obscure how much their interpretations are shaped by unspoken conventions involved in *writing* literary criticism."[11] We obscure how the practice we call reading is an explanatory method. This method is craftwork in a literal sense. It is something one does or makes with one's hands, and its mode of attention is a kind of dexterity. The "reading" is typed or in some few cases handwritten. To the degree to which information comes in from the eyes to the mind, it also goes out through the fingers to the screen or the page. To understand close reading as a method, therefore, we might want to turn our model from concentrated eyeing to hands-on immersion. That might give us a better sense of the kind of knowledge that critics both possess and make.

*   *   *

Let me begin with in-sentence quotation. This is the practice of placing language from the text one is discussing inside the sentence one is writing in such a way that accommodates the formal economy of each.[12] When critics quote in this fashion, they fold language they are writing about into language that is theirs. As with every other feature of close reading, this practice is not something we reflect much on explicitly, but it is steeped in norms of perspicuity, elegance, and evidence—norms of explanation that govern any field of study even as they vary according to field of study.[13] I want to know how our practices of in-sentence quotation advance arguments, and that means I want to know what epistemic claims attach themselves to the ability to sustain person, tense, and other features of syntax across two orders of writing.

Like most intensive handiwork, in-sentence quotation is a difficult thing to do. To attach more than a single word to your own, after all, is to accommodate an indissoluble grammatical epoxy; it is to adjust one's expression to the constraints of mood, number, person, and tense that belong to words grouped in an order. When, for example, Mary Favret wants to show how William Cowper includes in his domestic seclusion the sense of war happening at a distance, she begins with the framework set by eight words across two lines from his long poem *The Task*: "The noisy arrival of the post-boy intrudes upon the 'Winter Evening,' where the poet hopes to cobble out of 'undisturb'd retirement, and the hours / Of uninterrupted ev'ning' a rural retreat from hostile weather and imperial hostilities."[14] Consider the intuitive virtuosity shaping this moment from the everyday life of the discipline. Cowper's slightly out-of-balance parallelism forms a long prepositional phrase joined to the critic's own "where the poet hopes" by the silent ligature of a quotation mark. Favret's construction respects the grammatical and emotional mood set for it by Cowper's syntax yet nudges the picture of evening's fireside so that a soft presence of violence abroad somewhat disturbs the calm. The sentence "alerts us to unquiet" (59). What follows is dramatic and deft. Favret spins her words across and over three lines from Cowper, whose grammar acts as a binding warp for the whole:

If, while gathered with friends by the fireside, he reviews in "mem'ry"

> The dangers we have 'scap'd, the broken snare
> The disappointed foe, deliv'rance found
> … life preserv'd and peace restor'd,

his daily anticipation of the newspaper belies the security of these past participles. (60)

Note the performance. Cowper's three lines set the limits for what Favret may write about them. She has to make the "if" clause and the "daily anticipation" subject fit the contents of the memory at either end. As she does so, she discloses something about the poem. Favret's conditional statement holds across the entire sentence, but it encases the speaker's long indicative phrase in such a way that the past tense jostles uneasily with the expectation of what might be to come. Her words bind to the words of the poem to create a sense of temporal and felt disturbance amid a scene of calm.

This reading of *The Task*, like any other, turns on how the critic quotes the poem. To look at its method is to see the ordinary science of the discipline up close. Favret works within what is given to her, attaching her words to an already-set grammar. In the process, she coaxes out of the poem a set of answers to questions she's interested in pursuing, in this case about literature and wartime.[15] Further examples range across the limitless topics of interest to criticism. When Christina Sharpe wants to describe how a branded mark in Toni Morrison's *Beloved* identifies a mother to her daughter, a present to its past, and both to a sense of what it means "to live in the wake" of slavery, she describes the daughter's wish to receive the same mark: "The mother's response to Sethe's request that she 'mark the mark on me too' is a slap because she knows what the mark means and she knows, and Sethe will come to know, that she is already marked."[16] Sharpe here sustains Morrison's play between "mark" as verb and "mark" as noun but turns what had initially been a piece of dialogue to a conjunctive phrase interpreting the daughter's question as a matter of Black being.[17] The spoken imperative slips behind a pronoun and in front of a verb so that the six words now mean what Sharpe understands Sethe's mother to understand them to mean, the condition of "staying in the wake" and doing "wake work" (14). Looking at older materials, Seeta Chaganti turns to several meanings of *oynement* for medieval writers interested in dance and the moving body: "Lydgate observes in an allegorical capacity that 'Oynement ys a soote thyng, And rhyt vertuous in werking To woundys cloos & ope also,' while Capgrave likens St. Gilbert's 'vertu' to an 'oynement' that must be stirred and rolled with tribulation in order to enhance its pungency."[18] A long phrase in Middle English syntax and diction buckles but remains within the sentence of criticism, as an account of the animated materials of medieval cosmology comes into view.

Getting in-sentence quotation like this right is something one learns to do and is therefore a skilled practice. So on a first pass, let us say that the epistemology of close reading is a subspecies of the epistemology of skill. There is knowledge that is manifest in the act of placing words just so, even as there is knowledge that comes from what one has placed. This is the stuff and substance of inquiry in the literary humanities, however miniature the skilled performance might seem in comparison to others. A correspondent in a Stephen Crane story becomes shipwrecked and remembers a poem about a soldier, suddenly relevant to his situation. Elisa Tamarkin wants to discover something about how and when "relevance" became a criterion of judgment, a topic of inquiry that moves from examples, like stories and poems, to parallel works of psychology, to the historical situations of each. She begins, however, by writing with Crane's words alongside her own. "And now the poem that mysteriously entered his head moved him to 'a profound and perfectly impersonal comprehension,' and he 'was sorry for the soldier of the Legion who lay dying in Algiers.' The poem is 'no longer merely a picture of a few throes in the breast of a poet, meanwhile drinking tea' but has become part of the correspondent's reality, a living thing no less so than the waves that 'suddenly raged out like a mountain-cat.'"[19] The first sentence shares Crane's tense, joining the "and now" to a past movement and sorrow switched in the second sentence for a more active, literary present.[20] The effect is to have the "living thing" of Crane's own story burst like its nested poem into the "reality" of the critic's prose now thrumming

in immediacy and presence. Tea drinking and likened-to moun-
tain cats exist at the same time and in the same world as the critic's
waves and correspondent's head. Crane's story becomes a parable
of relevance when Tamarkin insets its language on a well-timed
pause and jump.

The skilled practice of in-sentence quotation consists in embedding the words of another so that the apt form is something of a
weave. Quotation of this variety is of a different order from skilled
practices of block or between-sentence quotation. There quoted
and novel words abut each other as separate units, like grouted
tiles, the one noticing something about the other in terms distinct
and set off by mood, diction, number, and other markers that distinguish one linguistic situation from another. In both practices,
writing criticism is knowing how to do something and the knowledge exhibited a kind of know-how. For in-sentence quotation, the
know-how is that of weaving another person's words with your own
so you gently alter both, so that some sort of third space emerges in
the process of interpretation. For block or between-sentence quotation, the know-how is that of adjusting your own idiom so that it
reveals something about another's, either by way of contrast or connection. "Consider the plainness of another seventeenth-century
pastoral speaker," asks Paul Alpers and then terminates his sentence with a colon.[21] Four lines of George Herbert's "The Flower"
follow, printed as verse:

> And now in age, I bud again,
> After so many deaths I live and write;
> I once more smell the dew and rain,
> And relish versing. (254)

As block or between-sentence quotations go, this one is relatively economical and therefore easier to write about than its ampler siblings, ranging as they sometimes do into the hundreds of words. The formal features of interest to my argument remain the same. Alpers doesn't so much weave Herbert's words with his own as set them off by punctuation so he may begin with variance. His gloss distances and then turns to back to the quoted words. "This is pastoral because, in its imagery and sense of human powers—its vulnerability, its treasuring of the senses and its giving over the earlier fantasies of conquering heaven—the speaker accepts the likeness between himself and the flower that gives the poem its title" (254). In a manner characteristic of block quotation, the noticing on this occasion is fundamentally demonstrative and deictic: look at these lines, this moment; observe how they do this thing.[22] *This* is pastoral. The genre designation then serves the purpose of further placing at a distance the lines to which the critic points, now not only at a spatial and syntactic remove but encased as instances of a type. The two orders of language aren't woven. They're mortared. Pointing to the block allows Alpers to curl back to the individual lines, his continuous tenses animating Herbert's series of simple present actions in such a way that they reveal the plain pastoral earthiness of transient things.

Alpers gets Herbert and pastoral right while keeping his language separate, looking back across a grammatical threshold. Other versions of skilled quotation between sentences attempt to glide across that threshold by, as it were, fading or blending the grout. Timothy Yu, for example, blends in-sentence with block quotation to describe the "remembered landscape" of Fred Wah's transnational, Asian-Canadian sense of place.[23] Yu quotes seven lines of unpunctuated, grammatically estranged English, points, and then instructs his reader how to understand what he has pointed to by a subtle art of melding:

> Waiting for saskatchewan
> and the origins grandparents countries places converged
> europe asia railroads carpenters nailed grain elevators
> Swift Current my grandmother in her house
> he built on the street
> and him his cafes namely the "Elite" on Central
> looked straight ahead Saskatchewan points to it. (58)

Yu begins his reading of this block with a demonstrative but soon folds the words he distances into a marked and punctuated grammar. The move from pointing to gripping—from remove to fusion—echoes a pattern Yu wants us to discover in the verse itself:

> The effect of these opening lines is of a kind of zooming-in, as "origins grandparents countries places" converge on the small town of Swift Current, and then on the individual figure of "my grandmother in her house." In the following line, however, the focus shifts to the unnamed "he" who built the house, a shift that is reinforced with the "and him" that opens the next line. With this shift of subject, our angle widens again, taking in the cafés, the town, and returning in chiasmic fashion to Saskatchewan. (58–59)

Yu divides and apportions "these opening lines" so they enter his sentences as silently fixed parts of speech. Wah's spectral "origins grandparents countries places" is no longer a floating list but now

the compound subject of the verb that ends the line. Yu's incorporation of the line "zooms in" and then out, as it brings home the
shifting perspective, moving up to the list then out to the pronouns
and then out of the poem entirely to the unquoted rewording at
the end.

The reworded end to the gloss meanwhile lies somewhere between the embedding of in-sentence quotation and the deixis of
block. Yu writes in Wah's language while retaining his own tense
and person. This kind of quotation without quoting—the *sounding
like* or practiced mimicry of one's object of study—is another way
of smoothing the joint of one's own words and someone else's. Like
its sibling form in literature proper, critical free indirect discourse
of this variety is interpretive through and through. When Jane Austen's narrator sounds like her character Emma Woodhouse, she is
providing an account of Emma's thinking (its slight aggression or
resentment with respect to Jane Fairfax, for example). To get the
voice right is to get the thought right, in the sense that the narrator's third person sounds like and so provides a compelling interpretation of the character's first person.[24] Critical free indirect discourse is interpretive in this respect, too, and likewise hits or misses
its mark to the degree that the voice or, better still, the style is gotten right. This is, for example, Nicholas Dames writing about musi-
cality and the experience of time in George Eliot's *Daniel Deronda*.
How well does Deronda's appearance match the idea that the vi-
sionary Zionist Mordecai has created for him or someone like him?
Dames quotes Eliot in block between his sentences to answer:

But the long-contemplated figure had come as an emotional
sequence of Mordecai's firmest theoretic convictions; it had
been wrought from the imagery of his most passionate life; and

it inevitably reappeared—reappeared in a more specific self-asserting form than ever. Deronda had that sort of resemblance to the preconceived type which a finely individual bust or portrait has to the more generalised copy left in our minds after a long interval: we renew our memory, but we hardly know with how much correction.[25]

In what follows, Dames doesn't point to this passage or quote from it directly. He sets out where the passage ends, launched by a passive construction that allows the critic and author seemingly to speak at once. "The time between first and second appearances is given color by the uncertainty surrounding the second appearance: how close is it to the original, how much has it been altered, how accurate was our recollection?" (160). The silencing of agency in the opening clause makes it so the questions hover over and between two voices, as if they were almost but not quite the block continuing, without quotation marks, past its indents and into the main text. The first-person plural remains in place. Sound and rhyme move from the one to the other. We know that these are the questions Eliot wants us to consider because Eliot seems to be asking them.

Writing close to Eliot fades the turn to commentary so that it is almost imperceptible. One set of words abuts another, but the effect is of Eliot continuing to write and therefore to explain her work in the words of someone else. This form of unmarked or not quite quotation, in other words, gets us to grasp in Eliot's voice questions the critic would like to see answered. How does Victorian realism understand the limits of a reader's interest in a way that Wagnerian avant-gardism does not? By what means does the experience of duration encode for Eliot moral and political dilemmas of ethnicity? Deronda has in Eliot's words "a subdued fervour of sympathy," the consideration of which receives quotation in full:

> It had helped to make him popular that he was sometimes a little compromised by this apparent comradeship. For a meditative interest in learning how human miseries are wrought—as precocious in him as another sort of genius in the poet who writes a Queen Mab at nineteen—was so infused with kindliness that it easily passed for comradeship. Enough. In many of our neighbour's lives, there is much not only of error and lapse, but of a certain exquisite goodness which can never be written or even spoken—only divined by each of us, according to the inward instruction of our own privacy. (162–63)

The commentary that follows begins with unquoted yet literal repetition: "Enough—or too much." The "enough" that is inside Eliot's prose and, without quotation marks, at the beginning of Dames's gloss makes the "or too much" come from Eliot even as it sets up what Dames wants us to see, spun through a combination of deictic, free indirect, and in-sentence address. "Eliot's plenitude of description here finds itself faced with a problem of sufficiency— how much is just right to evoke a character?—and ends with a sudden, frustrated admission that extension is often both tiresome and beside the point; better to have said too little, perhaps, about that which cannot really ever 'be written or even spoken'" (163). Front-loading the sentence seems to create its own plenitude of description until the payoff after the semicolon. From that point, the clause no longer points to *Deronda*; it takes on and then embeds the novel's language, stitching the *Eliotic* to *Eliot* in order to reveal an ambivalence about the project of attending to psychology at large.

*   *   *

The examples I have chosen might be described as scenes from the everyday life of literary criticism. Every one of them uses skills that might go unnoticed because their purpose is not to draw attention, but rather to enact and enable an interpretive argument at hand. This is method in action rather than talk about method. I have wanted to shine a light on some of its specific features, and so to lay the groundwork for understanding how aptness of style and dexterity of quotation have epistemic significance, as ways of getting things right. I will have more to say about this significance in the following chapter. Before doing so, however, I want to address some question of scale. My argument has and will continue to be concerned with matters at the foundations of critical method. I have started and will remain with the micro-case and -level, including bedrock procedures of quoting or sounding like and so extending the language you're interpreting in the sentence that you're writing. Practice at the microscale, I will continue to argue, exhibits a kind of skilled handiwork that is at once knowledge bearing and knowledge creating. It is a way of treating materials in such a way that works within their limits, grapples with the quiddity of their form, their culture, and their history.

As the last two words indicate, however, not everything concerned with method or rationale occurs at the microscale. Every one of the examples I have looked at works with its materials to scale up the register of interest. The "jarring frankness" of Eliot's "Enough" is "partly formal and cognitive ... but also, and perhaps more disturbingly for Eliot, political and ethical," concerned with the alignment of interiority and ethnicity in Victorian England (163). From the formal to the cognitive to the political and ethical. This is a familiar and well-founded journey. Even the most literary of my cases—Alpers on Herbert—sorts individual words and lines within the larger class of pastoral poetry, just as Favret's deftness with Cowper brings out wartime sensibility at a gradation more abstract and inclusive than verse about news, or Sharpe's artistry with Morrison creates a framework for understanding "living blackness in the diaspora, in the still unfolding aftermaths of Atlantic chattel slavery," or Yu's stitching and stretching of Wah limns a Pacific Rim diaspora from lines on a small Canadian prairie town (2). Every one of my examples, in other words, grapples with the thisness of particular artifacts in order to derive from them some more capacious argument, set of concerns, or register of significance. I have wanted only to focus on the grappling because that is where method takes off. Or rather, that is where the method distinctive to the discipline takes off. Scaling up from the particular to the larger than one requires all kinds of skills that lie outside the scope of this book: skilled acts of research and abstraction, theory building, and historical-chronological argument. Some of these are shared with other humanities disciplines or even other units of the academy, some more specific to literary studies. My point in this chapter is that the practice that allows various procedures of scaling up to happen—the contact, grappling, and sample taking from the particular—is a certain way of writing. That practice is a baseline competence and method because it provides a way of understanding that cannot be achieved by other means. Without that kind of contact, whatever is gotten to at scale will look and will be different. This difference will mark a certain loss.

It is important to recognize that loss. As criticism moves to engage concerns that are of interest to a variety of disciplines, it opens itself to perspectives that come from other ways of understanding the world. These perspectives add to and are in turn nourished by the special knowledge derived from practice at the micro-level, from close reading, including the distinctive art of quoting well. There's no reason to give this up. Even scholarship that derives maximal energy from exogenous methods and approaches—work that is in that way interdisciplinary—might retain the skills and methods distinctive to one discipline while putting them in conversation with another. It seems in any case important to stress the point that practice at the micro-level creates distinctive and irreplaceable knowledge, and to do so now, at a moment when even defenders of the humanities, like Eric Hayot, claim that "the humanities should not be organized around the institutionalized disciplines," but rather conceived as a "single unit" with a common method across them.[26] To organize the humanities or the sciences around something other than "institutionalized disciplines" is simply to organize them around something other than understanding the world. It is also to capitulate to a program of austerity done under the fig leaf of innovation and impact. There are disciplines for a reason, for the plain matter that the sundry dominions of literature and music and economics and chemistry are each real and worthy of study yet none reducible to the other.[27] What would be lost in the event of close reading's passing would be the equivalent of what would be lost from any other field of study should its proprietary method vanish from the world: a way of knowing, a way of orienting oneself to objects of interest, a way of saying to others that this esoteric piece of social and physical reality calls out to us as worth our time. No rhetoric of innovative reform can get around that fact. The bleak institutional landscape that has emerged in the wake of COVID should make us more, not less, inclined to fight for an entire epistemology already under attack. The steep inequality among strata of the university system that the pandemic has both revealed and exacerbated should make us more, not less, inclined to recognize the importance of work done all the time, across the furthest reaches of the system.

My point is just that the distinctive disciplinary contribution of this work happens in ordinary, often unnoticed practices at the smaller scale of things. For the study of literature, this work is often in the skilled adjustment of one's words to another's. To make the point that this practice forms a method, however, requires an account of how skill relates to knowledge. The question for the next chapter, therefore, is how does one move from skilled adjustment to the words of someone else to stating truths about and with these words? To use Gilbert Ryle's categories, how does one move from "knowing *how*" to quote well to "knowing *that*" something is the case with what you have quoted?[28] To answer these questions would be to understand at least in some provisional sense the manner in which the writing we call reading both creates and describes a kind of knowledge. It would be to situate and understand an important piece of method.

Skilled Practice [CHAPTER THREE]

I brought up the ordinary language philosopher Gilbert Ryle at the end of the last chapter for a reason. Ryle's midcentury distinction between "knowing *how*" and "knowing *that*" stands at the beginning of a still-ongoing discussion of the epistemology of skill within Anglo-American philosophy, one that might sharpen our sense of what counts as truth in a disciplinary context.[1] For that reason I'm going to spend some time with philosophers in this chapter, but the idea is not to have them tell us how we work. It is to think with their discussion of skill as a way to understand inquiry in the literary disciplines. The epistemology of skill has several features relevant for understanding the activity of critical writing as a way of knowing. It asks: When is doing something well a skill, and how do skills pick out features of the world? What is the relation between being good at something and grasping what the thing consists in or brings about? These questions are germane for how we consider acts of embedding another person's language within your own or sounding like language you point to because they examine whether the act would count as a mode of understanding that language and its world of composition and reference. They are especially so because they emphasize the *activity* of understanding. Ryle's interest in social and linguistic practices shifts the location of knowledge from contemplating propositions to engaging what lies before you. His critics will challenge and muddy his fundamental demarcation in ways that I will argue are important for getting a grip on how close reading forms an explanatory method. The original connection between knowing and doing, however, establishes an important basis for recognizing the activity of composing sentences from sentences as a truth-bearing practice.

What kind of knowledge do skilled actions exhibit and create? According to Ryle's influential distinction, knowing how to do something is of a different order from knowing something to be the case, although no less important or meaningful for being so. In making this distinction, Ryle wants to pry skilled action loose from what he sees as the "intellectualist" mistake of presuming a shadow antecedent to it in the phantom space of the mind. "According to the legend," Ryle writes, "whenever an agent does anything intelligently, his act is preceded and steered by another internal act of considering a regulative proposition appropriate to his practical problem" (31). According to legend, that is, intelligent action like writing a sentence from a sentence begins with a prior act of ruminating over what you intend to write, getting whatever the idea might be right in your head. The performance of the intelligent act is merely the execution of a well-thought-out plan. But this legend, he says, is entirely wrong:

> What distinguishes sensible from silly operations is not their parentage but their procedure, and this holds no less for intellectual than for practical performances. 'Intelligent' cannot be defined in terms of 'intellectual' or 'knowing *how*' in terms of 'knowing *that*'; 'thinking what I am doing' does not connote 'both think-

ing what to do and doing it.' When I do something intelligently, i.e. thinking what I am doing, I am doing one thing and not two. My performance has a special procedure or manner, not special antecedents. (32)

The only thing before an intelligent act of one form or another is the capacity to do the act well that we refer to as skill. Skills are not easy to acquire. "We build up intelligent capacities by training" until we "exercise, care, vigilance [and] criticism" with every application (42). At the same time, the intelligence of intelligent capacities requires them to be put in action. What would it matter or mean for me to be a skilled carpenter if I never touched wood, a skilled critic if I never wrote a sentence? Thinking and doing are not two separate things. Every time one acts intelligently, the actual thinking is in the performance. Attention therefore turns to the expert manner of doing something well, not to facts and propositions that might regulate that doing. Expertise, skill, and knowing how exist in the action itself, in the special procedure of the performance, while skilled knowledge is a capacity one builds up with training. Ryle's quarrel with "intellectualist" approaches to mind and behavior—his staged turn away from a dualism of inner deliberation and outward expression—thus had the corollary effect of making some activity seem full of mind. He opened up for sustained attention the idea that skilled practice was knowledge bearing.

Even as Ryle wants to distinguish skilled practice from the knowing of facts and propositions, he wants to make clear that skill is epistemically rich, not mere habit. "Knowing *how*" is its own kind of knowledge. That argument will be revised and revisited by Ryle's critics, but the initial claim is especially germane to understanding close reading as a method particular to a field of study. "Knowing *how"* dwells in performance rather than reflection and therefore differs according to the various composition of the world. To make this point, Ryle asks us to consider a few skilled practices across the variety of life:

> The boxer, the surgeon, the poet and the salesman apply their special criteria in the performance of their special tasks, for they are trying to get things right; and they are appraised as clever, skilful, inspired or shrewd not for the ways in which they consider, if they consider at all, prescriptions for conducting their special performances, but for the ways in which they conduct those performances themselves. (48)

Deeply learned and virtuoso as the boxer's or the surgeon's performances are, they are nevertheless not considered if one considers consideration to be something that is distinct from the doing itself. And yet neither boxing nor surgery nor poetry nor salesmanship is done by rote. Each requires training. I cannot get in the ring with a pro or sell a vacuum cleaner to a stranger without spending some time getting up to speed on how to comport myself in the activity. To be trained in one thing, moreover, usually implies that one is not trained in something else. Skilled actions apply "special criteria" to "special tasks." To conceive of "knowing *how*" as a particular kind of knowledge is thus to imagine the world divided into particular domains: this sort of athletics, that kind of writing. At the same time, it is to imagine that expert performance gets something right within (and perhaps about) a particular domain. That is what defines it as epistemic and garners to it a kind of value, the value of being full of mind. Finally, to think of skill as the getting of something right is to imagine not just that it has value but that it should be judged worthy of value. The virtuosity of an intelligent practice—its intelligence—needs to be recognized for it to stand. How else would a writer or a boxer or a salesman shine as performing well were they not appraised for the specialness of their special performance? It thus falls on some group of experts or connoisseurs to give credence to the claim that one knows how to do something well.

We don't have to adjust this model too much to understand it as a picture of expert knowledge located in disciplines of study, each with its own methods and criteria of value. As elsewhere, expert practice in this context varies according to its particular objects and ends, whether that is understanding how procurement works for supply chains or epistolary narrative occurs in cuneiform. For humanistic disciplines, object dependence of this variety means that practice takes different shapes in relation to the assorted media of the arts: close reading for literary studies, close looking for art history, and so on. The skills particular to each practice vary according to the media at hand because they require one to make contact with whatever one wants to understand. Again, it makes no sense to be skilled in something one never does, and doing gets the hands dirty with different kinds of stuff. Media are particular, and so are methods. That is why there is no supra-method across the humanities let alone all the disciplines of knowledge. To get a reading right would accordingly be to apply our discipline's "special procedure or manner" to the medium of language and to be appraised as clever or inspired for doing so well. And yet of what precise sort is the knowledge gained or exhibited according to this picture of disciplinary practice? Is appraisal a species of verification? These are important questions to ask because they return to the subject of authority and rationale. It would be nice if our methods got things right in a way that told us something about our special world of literary texts and artifacts if not the larger world of which such texts and artifacts are a part. I will take a close look in a later chapter at how appraisal might or might not stand as a means to adjudicate truth claims across the disciplines. I'd like first to unravel further the idea that getting it right is a kind of knowledge.

Ryle's distinctive contribution to the epistemology of skill was to insist that knowing how to do something does not require the application of facts from the mind and yet is full of mind all the same. The special knowledge involved in getting something right is in the activity itself. Writing in the decade after Ryle, Michael Polanyi would say of the importance of skill in scientific discovery that "practical wisdom is more truly embodied in action than expressed in rules of action."[2] For Polanyi even more than Ryle, skilled action carries with it a suite of learned yet tacitly understood ways of manipulating the world. Skill is "as much an art of doing as it is an art of knowing," and it is "at the very heart of science" (54, 55). Polanyi will go on to sort adept movement at the smaller scale with sustained conclusions at a larger frame of reference, a project, as we'll see, still central to the philosophy of science.[3] The point I would stress here is that the art of knowing as he puts it is (again) not two things but one, not a thinking hard and then doing well, but a literally thoughtful action. The unanswered question is how to broaden our sense of "the art of knowing" so that it includes knowing how to do something along with knowing something to be the case. As I have described it, close reading makes a good candidate for this epistemology. Once we dispense with the idea that close reading is a type of reading, we can move away from the view that it involves an especially hard concentration on written words. Close reading wouldn't have to be guided by the phantom antecedent of ideas had when reflecting intensely on language. Rather, its truths would dwell in the writing itself, in the loop that includes vision and touch in the thoughtful activity of the fingers.[4]

Ryle's account of skill stops short of arguing that thoughtful activity of this kind amounts to a knowing of something to be the case. While knowing *how* refers to intelligent actions guided by skill, only knowing *that* refers to "the knowledge of true propositions or facts" (26). I know how to cook faro; I know that water boils at 212 degrees Fahrenheit; and so on. Skills are full of knowledge, but they don't pick out features of the world, exactly. Here might lie the limits of the Rylean picture for our current purposes: the distinction between knowing *how* and knowing *that* holds intelligent action at once to be epistemically rich and unable to do explanatory work. What we want instead, as Polanyi seemed to anticipate, is an account of method that would understand sentences of close reading to tell truths because of the competence of their assembly. For readings with embedded or adjacent quotations, this demand covers the gist of the entire sentence as well as the accuracy of the cited material. The quoted words in a sentence of criticism need to fit the words you attach to and around them. They also need to be correct pictures of words found elsewhere, neither misquoted nor quoted out of context.[5] One should get both right, but simple accuracy is not really the point. The quoted and original words need to fit in such a way that makes a claim about a topic of concern. This is the role for close reading in the practice of inquiry. It sets the truth conditions of sentences that contain words both inside and outside of quotation marks in terms of the already-existing shape of the encountered world, so the veracity of any inquiry depends on how well the performance is done.

The skill of the performer determines the quality of the performance. So much is the connection between skill and truth in any

domain of inquiry. I have meant only to highlight how that relation is manifest in the practice of written criticism, and I have attempted to do so by drawing out a set of tacit assumptions about
truth in particular. These may be summarized as follows: When a
critic quotes a work of writing in the act of having something to say
about it, we recognize that her words are or ought to be truthful in
the minimal sense of actually existing in the work she is quoting.
You can't just make stuff up. More than this, however, we recognize that her quoted words fit a sentence or set of sentences while
making a claim about some larger matter of interest, whether feelings of community in the Asian diaspora or the collective elements
of the pastoral genre. There, too, you can't just make stuff up. But
the constraints on what you can say do not merely concern the accuracy of quoted words. They concern, rather, the elegance of fit
between one's words and another's, between a claim and its grip
on the world. The quoted work limits what you can say about it because you have to match your words to its given shape and meaning.
This is especially so for the varieties of in-sentence quotation I began with in the last chapter, and in that way the practice can stand
as paradigmatic for the whole. Elegance is aptness, and aptness
elegance. One set of words is right for another when it fits more than
breaks their existing character. The same is the case in different degrees for deictic and indirect manners of quotation where acts of
pointing, looping back, or sounding like succeed because they are
precise in style or idea, because they are apt in the way they char-
acterize or echo or extend the words to which they are directed. For
criticism, saying something is the case about a set of words is therefore a very specific sort of assertion, the validity of which depends
on the quality of the form and the meaningfulness of the parts alike.
To break the form would be to strain the assertion. When we rec-

ognize a critic to make a valid claim about some larger matter of interest, we credit her with scaling up the argument from words to worlds by means of the apt treatment of the former. The question is how exactly does that happen? What is it that we credit and how does it work?

Considered in terms of the everyday life of literary criticism, the matter might be phrased like this: The apt placement of words made for the occasion among quoted words already connected is a kind of know-how, the truth expressed a kind of knowing that. What's the route from the first to the second? Some of the more recent and lively debates in the epistemology of skill have taken up just this problem. The so-called intellectualist response to Ryle, for example, insists, as Jason Stanley has put it, that "knowing how is a species of knowing that."[6] Stanley and philosophers like him mean to bring propositional and practical knowledge closer together so that to know how to do something is also to know that something is the case. The goal is to nudge Ryle's conception of the intellect so that intellectually guided action does not require a prior contemplative act of rumination and is not restricted to the mere gathering of facts. Intellection on this view comes to seem more active and is no longer "behaviorally inert" (26). Stanley's argument involves "deflating the notion of *contemplating a proposition*" and putting in its place the idea that "skilled action requires being directly guided by one's propositional knowledge—being guided automatically and without reflection" (22, 24). To transpose an imperative statement about the marks of slavery to an embedded consideration of the condition left in their wake is to work at once with words and their worlds of significance. The success at doing both would depend on being directed by what one knows about each. Skilled behavior comes to seem even more full of mind than it was in Ryle's picture, as deft craftwork now identifies, explains, and finally transforms elements of the encountered world. When one gets something right by following "the special criteria" of one's craft, one gets the activity and the thing right.

One has an idea of where to look and what to do, on this view, because one already has a store of knowledge about where to look and what to do. That store is just not contemplative. It is something more like a standing disposition, ready to be activated and improved with any immersion in the particular ecology of literary works and their surrounding cultures. To remain with my example from Christina Sharpe, the critic would know how to sift Morrison's words within her own because she knows that the experience and meaning of the Middle Passage have the features that they do. I will want to dissent from some dimensions of this account of the priority of intellect to practice and argue in its stead for a stronger unity between them. All the same, I think it is important to recognize how the focus on activity more than rumination, on the doing of such things as stitching words to words without breaking syntax, makes for a good understanding of close reading specifically. Appropriately deflated, the "intellect" of the "intellectualist" response to Ryle fits with the special kinesis of literary studies. Knowledge resides in the fingers doing the writing as much as the eyes doing the reading. Viewed this way, Ryle has too detached and contemplative a view of propositional thinking. He "over-intellectualizes the intellect itself," as Alva Noë has put it, despite his invaluable attention to skill as laden with mind.[7] He puts too great a distance between knowing about a matter of interest and knowing how to do something, even as he wants to make know-how an epistemically respectable sphere of life. The point is relevant to literary criticism because it helps to answer our question concerning what we credit when we credit a critic's knowledge. When we do so, we credit her knowing how to make something from words *because* she knows about what she has put together and revealed.

We might ask, however, whether this view of things puts too much emphasis on this "knowing about" dimension to criticism. The idea that skill is intellectually guided action seems to put propositional knowledge in advance of its encounter with the world and so, as Carlotta Pavese has argued, to "prioritiz[e] knowledge over skills in the order of explanation."[8] To conceive of literary critical know-how as merely the putting into practice of a standing body of knowledge would be an unfortunate reduction. Favret would begin knowing something about Cowper, wartime, and clauses, and then bring that knowledge to her dexterity with his language. Dames would begin with ideas about ethnicity in Victorian England before writing in the manner of Eliot. Even this "intellectualist" construal seems finally a poor description of the way critics provide an account of Cowper or Eliot or Morrison and their worlds in the act of writing itself. When we credit what critics are doing, we don't just notice their arguments. We attribute the success of their arguments to the virtuosity of their practice. Practical knowledge, in other words, is itself a domain of the intellect, as much for literary criticism as for any other discipline or sphere of life. Favret's, Sharpe's, and Dames's points, after all, hold in precisely the way they have ordered their sentences: the conditional warping of Cowper's indicative to reveal disquiet; the mood shifting of dialogue to draw being across generations; the having Eliot herself seem to ask questions about music and ethnicity. We would be hard-pressed to distinguish or extract the argument from the composition in any one of these examples. Nor should we have to. This is one consequence of close reading being in actual fact a practice of writing.

The argument is in the act and shape of the performance, not prior to it in some state of fact or proposition.

Arguments in criticism may of course be paraphrased or summarized, as I have just attempted to do, but the paraphrase or summary depends on the way the performance is done, as it is the performance and not the paraphrase or summary that gets it right. The first is epistemically as well as temporally prior to the second. The truth of whatever is before the reading is not simply there for the critic to discover; it requires the active coaxing and commingling of the critic's words for it to take shape. So much is borne out in the work culture of the discipline. Consider the manner in which scholars in the literary humanities present their arguments at conferences and lectures. While it is now customary to accompany talks with PowerPoints, rarely if ever do critics extemporize over bullet-pointed slides as do their colleagues in analytic philosophy or most of the social sciences. The live presentation of literary criticism tends instead to be read out word for word from printed or digital copy, and that is because the argument is understood to be inseparable from the writing. The art of extemporizing over bullet points, in contrast, consists in abstraction from the material under consideration. These are different practices aligned with distinct methods suited to various disciplines. Each is a skill in its own right, and only by contortion could the one be made to fit the other. Only by contortion, to introduce another example, could Santanu Das's argument that *Across the Black Waters* (1939), Mulk Raj Anand's novel of Indian soldiers during the First World War, shows a "double ambivalence" of the soldiers toward the Raj and the author toward the soldiers be rendered as layered and dotted sentence fragments.[9] Each extracted and stacked assertion would lose its grip on the "pile-up of clauses, twisting and turning through 'because,' 'but,' 'though' and the accretive intensity of commas," and "the ebb and flow of feeling" of a "local, ingrown, and intensely felt" consciousness stretched between South Asia and France would fade from view (346). Even the finest lineation of a reading on bullets could do no more than point to a performance elsewhere. The practice of reading sentence by sentence maintains the link between inserted and surrounding words that constitutes the argument itself.

I take the reluctance to abandon this practice as evidence of its epistemic significance. To return to my present concerns, it indicates that the shuttling of the intellect to practice that happens in the revision to Ryle does not go far enough, at least with respect to our understanding of close reading. What we want is an account of know-how that describes the creation and discovery of truths in the activity itself, whatever that might be, so that what is "gotten right" is at one and the same time some sort of method and some feature of the world. The second should rely on the first. An "apt performance," as Ernest Sosa has put it, is "accurate because adroit," "true because competent."[10] Some feature of the encountered world comes into view better because some agent has what Sosa calls the "virtue" to handle it with dexterity and care.[11] In-sentence quotation is exemplary in this respect because it is a practice of skilled embedding, whose claims for truth follow from an apt negotiation with and adjustment to (again) the indissoluble grammatical epoxy before you. But other forms of quotation and adjacent varieties of close reading do the same kind of work insofar as each is a medium and situation-specific adjustment of style and address to what lies before them. Remove that skill and you lose the idea, not because the idea has no way to enter the world of visible things, but rather because skilled practice is the idea itself. The aptness of the performance—its method—just ensures that the idea has been gotten right. Anyone can come up with something interesting to say. Few can embody something interesting in practice.

Few can do so because methods are particular to domains of training and embodied skill. For criticism as well as chemistry, that is the domain of an academic discipline, but the point holds across the sundry varieties of practice inside and outside the university. "Knowledge and skill" play a central role in "opening up the world of experience," writes Noë, because we only "achieve access to the world around us through skilled engagement; we acquire and deploy the skills needed to bring the world into focus."[12] Academic disciplines are special only because they bring the world into focus with the goal of creating and disseminating knowledge by means of teaching and research. They are loci of inquiry designed to make the world intelligible, a distinctive kind of focus. I have argued that the skill particular to literary critical inquiry takes a broad and eclectic form, but that its foundation includes shared and medium-specific practices at the microscale. Apt quotation, for example, serves inquiry in the literary humanities because it builds a lattice that may be scaled up to larger matters of interest. Readings are apt because they are adroit, and they are scalable because they are apt. A well-formed latticework embeds or points to or sounds like the words of the world in such a way that supports inquiry ranging as widely as critical interest may go. In Das's reading of Anand, this interest extends all the way to "the multiple and intersecting histories of race, class, war, social relations and empire" built on "a nerve-centre and a micro-history" of literary character (347, 351). But it needn't do so. Inquiry will range as it does, near and narrow as well as far and wide. In the everyday life of that happening, however, it is skill that supports the inquiry by providing the ground and authority to make the claims one does, no matter what they are.

This is surely the case for all disciplines of knowledge, as well as every other walk of life where it is important that work is done well for it to be sound. The only special feature of the disciplines is the goal they have to explain and so transform the world. I used the metaphor of latticework and the idea of ground to emphasize that skill works in the concrete, as a kind of grappling with a medium of concern. My point was to underscore that the literary disciplines are at bottom an empirical enterprise. They make claims about the encountered world. That much of course makes them akin to a science. "Science is epistemically efficacious because it is especially empirical."[13] This is a philosopher of science, Michael Strevens, writing in the roughly contemporary moment. The point is, of course, familiar. "The defining characteristic of an empirical statement," writes Carl Hempel in the first sentence of one of the twentieth century's foundational works in the philosophy of science, "is its capability of being tested by a confrontation with experiential findings."[14] There is little to contest in this view, so long as we add that science is efficacious with respect to its domain because it is especially empirical in comparison to other ways of understanding that domain, such as alchemy or astrology. By pointing to medium-specific skills in humanistic method, I am arguing for *their* especially empirical relation to domains not covered by the natural or social sciences. Literary critical skill is empirical in a way that is required by its medium. We can see this vividly in quotation where the medium pushes back and shapes what you can do with it in any one instance. The skill of criticism is just to reach out to the world in such a way that the grasp holds.

Criticism is empirical because it tracks and responds to the materials it endeavors to understand, because its limitless inquiries proceed from the limits of these materials. To put it this way is to return to the idea of close reading as handiwork, with special emphasis on how the practice creates something from the materials it works with and so transforms as it explains the world. I hope this relieves any worries that may linger around the very idea of empirical grounds and commitments. Criticism is not simply the amassing of facts. If it were, then it wouldn't matter what form the engagement with other people's words took. The facts of the matter could simply be scooped up once collected. If the examples show anything, however, it is that the skilled practice of writing about writing makes something new in the act of interpreting it. It is fundamentally and irreducibly a creative act. The pattern set down in front of you only provides the enabling constraints for how you go about asking and answering questions of interest along with the background conditions for how others appraise your performance. I now turn to the nature of that creativity and that appraisal.

CHAPTER FOUR

Interpretation and Creativity

I have argued that method in literary criticism is to be found in practice rather than ideas about practice and that truth in literary criticism derives from hands-on engagement with texts rather than facts or assertions about them. I have looked at practices of quotation in particular because quoting a work of writing is about as hands-on as you can get. To quote is, as it were, to touch someone else's words and then weave them within or place them alongside your own. Not all varieties of closeness follow these exact paths, of course. I drew attention also to critical mimicry, or writing in free indirect style, and in the present chapter I will look at practices of interpretive plot summary. In all cases, however, I have wanted to emphasize how critics mold and shape the object they analyze, so that what spools out in any given sentence of criticism is a composite made to answer a question at hand. I have argued that this act of shaping is creative, a making of something new and something valuable.[1] I'd like to spend more time with that now.

Universities tend to divide departments that teach the making of things from departments that teach their analysis, a department of art history from a school of fine arts and so on down the line.

Literature departments are somewhat anomalous in this respect because they often contain units or programs devoted to creative writing, each with its own protocols for judgment and paths through the major or toward an MFA. The reason for this anomaly can be extended to the whole of literary studies and considered central to its rationale. Practitioners in the discipline work in the same linguistic medium as their objects and so commingle with what they analyze. I've mentioned the significance of this simple fact from time to time. It is worth special attention now as we consider the relation between making and knowing in literary studies. I'm going to argue that the creative and epistemic dimensions of critical writing cannot be separated, that we know because we make and make in order to know. Medium coincidence is central to this fact.

The idea that interpretation involves making as well as understanding is itself not new. In broad form, creativity has long been understood as an integral part of critical method, especially when attention turns to the inter-involvement of one's own words and someone else's. For this reason, it was of special concern to hermeneutics as that version of literary study took shape in the nineteenth and twentieth centuries. In *Hermeneutics and Criticism* (1838), for example, the foundational text in the field, Friedrich Schleiermacher defines hermeneutics as the "art [*Kunst*] of understanding particularly the written discourse of another person correctly."[2] *Kunst* is German for the fine arts as well as skilled craftsmanship, and Schleiermacher uses the term deliberately. To understand the written discourse of another person correctly, in one's own written discourse, is to put oneself in the linguistic and psychological circumstances of that person. The "art" of hermeneutics is therefore a delicate procedure of reconstruction: building up from individual phrases, ideas, sentences, beliefs, and works to the minds and languages of which they are a part, returning with added knowledge to where one began, and then starting anew.

This movement from part to whole and back draws the hermeneutic circle.[3] What is of particular interest to the current argument is that Schleiermacher views the drawing of the circle as an aesthetic practice, *eine Kunst*, in manner if not outcome. "The complete task of hermeneutics is to be regarded as a work of art, but not as if carrying it out resulted in a work of art, but in such a way that the activity only bears the *character* of art in itself, because the application is not also given with the rules, i.e. cannot be mechanised" (11). Unlike grammar or chemistry, hermeneutic reconstruction does not follow an exact formula, and like poetry or fiction, it relies on the flair and dexterity of a maker, someone who by application immerses herself in thought and language. Hermeneutics "depends on the talent for language and the talent for knowledge of individual people"—a "living awareness"—because it is an inventive practice of intermixing within a single medium (11). It extends the "character of art" over three folds: "the art of presenting one's thoughts correctly" and so also "the art of communicating someone else's utterance to a third person" and, as a consequence, "the art of understanding another person's utterance correctly" (5). The elegance of a hermeneut's presentation holds pride of place, but the triple art of interpretation is only complete when the correct understanding moves "as the mediator" from one scholar to another and back, limning the hermeneutic circle at large (5). Each arc of the circle has to be at once "correct" and artful, a talented absorption of another's words among your own that is then recognized by someone else. The result is a "better understanding" or even "complete knowledge," but the whole has to be done well and gotten right (24).

Schleiermacher's understanding of scholarly community and the significance of talent occurs well before the advent of university culture as we currently understand it. Yet the link he draws among creativity, knowledge, and medium persists and is important; in fact, it persists because it is important to the inner logic of literary study as a discipline. "In a certain sense, interpretation probably is re-creation," Hans-Georg Gadamer writes more than a century later, and then adds in a slight reordering of Schleiermacher, "a re-creation not of the creative act but of the created work, which has to be brought to representation in accord with the meaning the interpreter finds in it."[4] Gadamer attends to the artifactual end rather than the active making of critical sentences because he is concerned with the way interpretation bends works of writing toward topics and questions at hand. As with the philosophers of the last chapter, we need not subscribe to all of Gadamer's larger project to notice what is especially relevant to understanding criticism. The goal of the talented hermeneut is not so much to re-create the circumstances in which a work was written as to place aspects of the work within a field of inquiry. And to do that, the hermeneut has to make the work present in such a way that responds to her specific interests.[5] Seen this way, each one of the examples from earlier chapters of this book, and any example an informed reader might think of on her own, is of a text bent by appropriately partial designs. Writing about the sense of war in *The Task* brings out just one dimension of a long and multifaceted poem, but such "accord" would hold even if the poem were shorter and simpler. Writing about a mark in *Beloved* alights on just one moment to ask about survival in the wake of devastation, just as music in *Daniel Deronda* pitches inquiry in a direction that might have gone otherwise (toward marriage or boating, say). In each case and in any other, "the fact that the representation is bound to the work is not lessened by the fact that this bond can have no fixed criterion" (123). Some statements lie beyond the joint limits of grammar and culture, but it does not follow that a single or even finite set of readings are all that's allowed. "There is something absurd about the whole idea of a unique, correct interpretation" because interpretation happens in the process of making one thing from another (123). The critic brings the work to representation as she binds her words to its words, asking whatever questions fit the inquiry, her creativity as absolute as it is restricted. All interpretation composes something new within the constraints of what it is given.

The practice of in-sentence quotation I spent some time with earlier is distinctive and special because it so demonstrably embodies the re-creating act, in which a new object emerges from the apt spinning of two orders of language. What is required for the spinning to be apt is that it "be accurate because adroit, successful because competent."[6] In-sentence quotation demonstrably embodies this quality because it puts the limits and spurs to creativity so clearly in view as nothing less than units of composition itself. The explanandum becomes in actual, literal fact incorporated as expressive parts of the explanation. Once again, literary criticism is unique among interpretive practices in this regard, a crucial and relatively unexamined feature of the discipline I have referred to as medium coincidence. Art historians don't paint about painting nor do musicologists write music about music. This is of course not to say that literary criticism is the only creative discipline in the interpretive humanities, just that its ordinary mode of creativity depends on sharing a medium with its object.[7] Art historical writing and criticism along with other forms of film and media studies, in contrast, have ekphrastic modes of explanation whose method and creativity depend on translating features of nonverbal artifacts into the language of academic argument. Their practice involves an unavoidable and intricate shift from one medium to another. "Art history," writes the art historian Jas Elsner in uncompromising terms, "is nothing other than ekphrasis, or more precisely an extended argument built on ekphrasis."[8] It endeavors to turn its object "from a thing that signifies by volume, shape, visual resonance, texture into one that speaks within the structures of grammar, language, verbal semiotics" (12). The turn is inevitable and inevitably partial to the interpretive schema at hand; it entices "the non-verbally responsive object into a state where it is both available as ekphrasis and so angled in its new descriptive form as to be appropriate to the specific argument being made" (13). This is a notable and important difference from the interpretive procedures specific to the study of literature. To be available as ekphrasis involves a sort of annihilation and rebirth, whereas to be available as quotation or deixis or imitation involves a sort of perseverance into a new shape.

As with quotation and its kin, any ekphrastic description of art might always have taken another angle had the desires of the art historian been other than what they were. Ekphrasis both creates a "parallel work of art" to the one under discussion and is the only way to bring the latter into a field of inquiry (12). Its ordinary mode of creativity just depends on not sharing a medium with an object. Ekphrastic interpretation is apt or not according to norms specific to art history and its silent means of estimating whether the cross-medial transit has gone right. I have drawn this out because I have wanted, by way of contrast, to point to the importance of medium coincidence for the creative and epistemic dimension to literary studies. You can't turn a work of literature or art into an object of knowledge without bringing it into your own writing, and you can't do *that* without getting the object to fit, aptness and knowing being inseparable. Only in the study of literature, however, does the raw material of the work enter into and define the scope of the sentence itself. To know something in the field is to meld, mesh, and turn something while maintaining its medium.

The importance of this kind of incorporation can be further illustrated by comparing literary studies to other disciplines that work on language. There the fact of medium coincidence produces a rebound in the opposite direction, from integration to estrangement. Consider the following example from a recent article in a field-leading journal in the discipline of linguistics. The author wants to examine what happens when a predicate phrase gets elided in response to an indicative sentence. One person says, "Mary has dated someone," and another responds, "Who?" As that occurs, an implied "Who has Mary dated?" gets shortened in an act of "headless ellipsis" that moves the stranded "who" (the head of the phrase) to an interrogative position. Only certain kinds of heads can move like this, but why that is the case is a puzzle. We may express the headless ellipsis and so get a grip on the puzzle, the author argues, as follows: "$[_{CP}$ who$_i$ C$_{[Q,wh]}$ $[_{TP}$ Mary$_k$ $[_{T'}$ has$_j$ $[_{AuxP}$ t$_j$ $[_{vP}$ t$_k$ dated-v $[_{VP}$ t$_V$ t$_i]]]]]$."[9] What has happened in the analysis? The marks formalize a linguistic situation, but they aren't exactly language.[10] They have shape, shade, and meaning but can neither be spoken nor quoted. It seems the aim of bringing the marks to the argument is not so much to translate or embed them in the writing as to make language a thing expressed in a notational form requiring the linguist's training to understand. Or consider this example from a recent prize-winning article in the philosophy of language. How are we to understand the intricate way that context distinguishes the meaning of "cut" as "sever in horizontal pieces" when someone is mowing the lawn from "sever in vertical pieces" when someone is slicing a cake? We may begin to get an answer, the author proposes, when we view the operation as "$[[cut]]^c_M = mod(cut, c)([[cut]]^c)$" and then "$= [\lambda P_{<e,<e,t>>}.\lambda x.\lambda y.P(x)(y) \wedge \text{IN PIECES}(x)]([[cut]]^c)$" and finally "$= \lambda x.\lambda y.\text{CUT}(x,y) \wedge \text{IN PIECES}(x).$"[11] Once again, we are in the presence of a linguistic situation but not the presence of language. The marks abstract the logical structure of each utterance from quotation or speech. They have no idiom or sound and cannot be imitated.

The more linguistics and the philosophy of language want to understand their linguistic objects, the more their mode of expression moves away from them. In the event, they move out of language entirely to something else. Words themselves give way to formal or logical notation, in a kind of reverse ekphrasis taken to the extreme. The extremity of this distance has the air of objectivity and science, a view from nowhere that defines what it means to argue and to know. I don't intend to challenge this view, which may or may not be appropriate to linguistic objects as they are understood by other disciplines. I do intend to establish the contrasting practice of the literary humanities, where the closer you are, the better you argue and the more you know. We may summarize the disciplinary situation with respect to language therefore as follows: Other humanistic disciplines convert their nonverbal objects into language to make them close, while other language-oriented disciplines shuck their medium to establish distance. Only the literary disciplines sustain closeness and medium at once.[12]

The point is simple but not mundane. The ordinary science of literary studies works with the same linguistic material as its objects. That is why quotation plays a more important role there than in the other humanistic disciplines, let alone the social and natural sciences. And that is also why the interpretive act of criticism is inescapably creative. The epistemic virtue of a given reading cannot be separated from its making of something from the very material being discussed. To emphasize the creative dimension of literary studies therefore does nothing to lower its claim to truth of this or that kind. In fact, it begins to provide an account of that claim.

* * *

Now is perhaps the time to own up to and celebrate creativity in literary criticism. It has long been sensed if only fitfully embraced. Consider a moment closer in our rearview mirror than either Schleiermacher or Gadamer. When Geoffrey Hartman starts to puzzle over his manner of mixing his own words with the words of others, he describes the practice as "both creative and thoughtful," neither one more than the other.[13] The closeness of critical writing, he recognizes, blurs the line between text and commentary and thus is a kind of art form. "The line of exegesis" is as "precariously extensible as the line of the text," each wrapping itself around the other (206). To write criticism is to make something new, to create "texts—a literature—of its own" (213). At the same time, to think about literature is also to write about it in its own materials. Thought happens in that practice itself. One cannot think about literature, Hartman argues, without the creative practice of writing about literature. The work of linguistic interposition is at once aesthetic and epistemic, craft and knowing.

This distinction appears in Hartman's work as an unresolved tension between creative freedom and hermeneutic integrity, each held within a single practice of writing. Recognizing the inventive dimension to "writing about literature," as he puts in one of his balder formulations, means worrying about the analytic dimension to the same (162). Keeping the two apart then allows for the drama of their reintegration. Does the new object made from interpretive engagement float free from what it is supposed to interpret? Is criticism now at a unique stage in its relation to its objects? These questions are posed with some to-do. "The circle of understanding encompasses both the interpreter and the given text; the text, in fact, is never something radically other except insofar as it is radically near" (167). To write about something is at once to render it an object of study and at the same time to draw it into one's language; it is to make it both strange and close. Hartman concludes, "The question What is disclosed by reading? invokes therefore a double text that remains a hendiadys: the text referred to by the interpreter, and the text on the text created by the referring act of criticism" (167).

This is a notable selection of trope. In classical rhetoric, the figure of hendiadys substitutes a relation of equivalence between two parts of speech for a prior relation of subordination.[14] In the place of a noun modified by an adjective, for example, hendiadys puts two nouns joined by a conjunction: "pain and suffering" replaces "painful suffering," and so on. Hartman evidently wants to use this figural shift to equality among formerly stratified parts of speech as a model for picturing a new equivalence between critical and literary texts. The two would be linked but separate, held together by the very melodrama of reference that preoccupied his theoretical generation. That melodrama at once raises the stakes and clouds the insight. What Hartman describes after all is not two separate but equal texts; it is the single work that joins the two. There is only the text created by criticism. Cleared of the fanfare of reference, in other words, a quieter end can be heard, namely, that knowing and creating have a peculiar and medium-specific bond in literary criticism. It is because they share the same medium that criticism can, in Hartman's phrase, "elaborate" on literature. It is because he writes about writing that the "texts that course through" him can seem "to be accompanied by a will to analysis that makes them stutter" (177). To begin where another stutters is to add words where another's stop and then to stop so another may continue. The metaphor uses speech to describe writing, as the metaphor of close reading uses reading to do the same. Unlike reading, however, stuttering is an "elaboration" within the linguistic medium of what is before you. The idea is less heated, but (I think) it gets a better handle on the way literary critical "analysis" adds to, subtracts from, and otherwise works with what gets analyzed. To write sentences of criticism is to work with what it is given, in its materials.

The practices of quotation I've been discussing are just this analysis in motion, instances of the largely unnoticed because after a time intuitive skill that puts substance to the idea that writing criticism creates something in the act of interpreting it. One imagines that Hartman had a sentence like this one in mind when he pictured himself filling in the stuttered speech of someone else: "When Wordsworth opens 'Tintern Abbey' with 'Five years have past; five summers with the length / Of five long winters! and again I hear …,' the drawn-out words express a mind that remains in 'somewhat of a sad perplexity,' a mind that tries to locate in time what is lost, but cannot do so with therapeutic precision."[15] This unremarkable sentence from the collection *The Unremarkable Wordsworth* manages to fold the first two lines of "Tintern Abbey" into Hartman's prose without straining the syntax of his opening clause and then to add a third line on the feeling of the mind's revival from considerably later in the poem. To do this, Hartman's Wordsworth stutters at the second line, before he can complete his sentence by saying that again he has heard "These waters, rolling from their mountain-springs / With a sweet inland murmur."[16] Hartman avoids the awkward redoubling of his own prepositional phrase with Wordsworth's even as he sustains the fit between his and the poem's words on each side of the quotation. Like a seasoned gardener, Hartman knows how to graft the lines from "Tintern Abbey" precisely where the prepositional phrase slides into its subject. Wordsworth's own preposition lies pruned on the ground, as Hartman coaxes the poem to reveal a sense of enigmatic loss. The virtuosity of the pruning and the splicing is that they at once seem apt and go unnoticed, designed to answer questions Hartman had about the varieties of consciousness explored in the Romantic lyric. Does the sentence assert a truth? It seems peculiar to ask this, but the answer I think is, yes, of course it does. There is an implicit "it is true that" hovering over the sentence, as there is in almost all criticism. To say "it is true that, when Wordsworth opens 'Tintern Abbey,'" and so forth, would seem peculiar because saying so doesn't add anything to the rest of the sentence. The rest of the sentence remains true or false in virtue of its aptness to compel our assent, our appraisal of it as well-formed, perspicuous, or adroit.[17]

Hartman's practice was in this way ahead of his theory. His skill was to make something new by using parts of what he was studying in the inquiry itself, using, as I've said, the explanandum in the act of explanation. Viewed in that manner, the drama of integrating creativity with thoughtfulness fades. A similar but distinct act of creativity occurs when critics need to call up narrative dimensions of a work in order to place the work within a field of inquiry. This is the familiar but not so often discussed art of interpretive plot summary, the quick going-over of select narrative context in the service of some larger analysis and argument. When, for example, Anne Whitehead wants to discuss how Kazuo Ishiguro's *Never Let Me Go* dramatizes and gives form to tensions within the aesthetics of empathy, she begins with a quick synopsis: "Narrated by thirty-one-year-old Kathy H., the novel looks back to her life at the boarding school of Hailsham and the close friendships that she developed there with her fellow schoolmates Tommy and Ruth. The education at Hailsham is firmly rooted in the arts, with the students regularly producing artworks and reading literature, with a particular emphasis on the Victorian novel."[18] This seems like a plain description of events, but in actual fact Whitehead has compressed and ordered the story so that the novel's investment in the arts is central to its treatment of caregiving. She is interested in complicating the recourse to empathy that some have made as a defense of the humanities, and her summary selects from aspects of the narrative that make it especially relevant to the meta-aesthetic point about the value of teaching and reading fiction. As with quotation, the compression and the ordering of the plot could always have gone otherwise within limits placed by the work itself. *Never Let Me Go* might be told as an allegory about race or a reflection on counterfactual history but not as a consideration of the wool industry or video gaming. The summary is itself a story written in miniature, drawn from the larger pile of events in the unstated background.

Acts like these occur all the time in the course of critical writing, not just in introducing works but at any point one needs to gather and tilt the work before making contact with it. This is again a medium-specific sort of making because it composes with elements of time and modality that are particular to language. The summarizing critic doesn't quote, point to, or imitate the language of the text, however, so much as narrate from it, stitching events in causal and temporal relation suited to the inquiry. On such occasions, the creative relation between the summary and the larger narrative might be illuminated by the familiar narratological distinction between *syuzhet* and *fabula*, where *syuzhet* refers to the form of the events in their actual presentation within the work (how the story is told), and *fabula* the background totality imagined to include these events in their proper order.[19] The *syuzhet* is the creatively formed object one reads, and *fabula* the formless whole it projects. Interpretive plot summary works in similar fashion by placing the formed work of the novel in the formless background of the summary while supplying form to its chosen version of events. In her reading of Nevil Shute's *On the Beach*, for example, Sharon Marcus summarizes the novel in order to examine styles of living with the knowledge of imminent death. The novel itself concerns a long moment in which nuclear wars in one part of the world will or will not destroy life in another. How does life go on in the meantime, before it is likely to end for everyone? "*On the Beach* begins with its characters in acute uncertainty. They know that radiation from nuclear weapons is heading toward the southern hemisphere but not when or even if it will arrive. Several characters hope the radiation may dissipate as it travels, and the novel lends their optimism some credence, as radio transmissions from Seattle introduce the possibility that radiation sickness is survivable."[20] Marcus's elegantly clipped sentences move with little embroidery or interruption over incident, consequence, and represented emotion. One story emerges from another in the service of a third. The design is to focus on a perhaps unexpected response to doom. As their fate becomes clear, "the majority of the novel's characters cope by attaching themselves to everyday life: they organize picnics, repair fences, plant flowers" (451). This is a kind of mini-narrative fashioned from the novel's more capacious sequence of events, a meta-*syuzhet*, or story of a story, that turns the novel itself into *fabula*. Something like this happens every time one summarizes in the service of inquiry. The creative act of making form tilts the plot for explanatory ends. Marcus designs her story for "understanding mortality and everyday life in more ordinary circumstances" than the end of the world and to explore in particular how "people facing death will attach themselves all the more fiercely to the mundane" (451). It is again important that one doesn't just make stuff up. In fact, Marcus faults other readers for getting some of the events or reflections in the novel wrong (450). Accuracy in this respect is, however, the ground for apt reconstruction to interpretive ends. She goes on to support her argument concerning the dying's attachment to the mundane with research from other disciplines, but the literary critical insight contributes something on its own, a truth conveyed in the act and aptness of summary, a truth available only because of the creative act.

* * *

Ten years after the 2008 financial crisis, the number of tenure-track jobs in English would drop by 55 percent.[21] In the years after COVID, the market as we knew it would disappear. Amid all of this, the only subfield to experience an aggregate increase in advertised jobs would be creative writing. Between 2009 and 2019, the number of its tenure-track ads increased by 12 percent, and its share of the discipline's hiring doubled.[22] The current situation is radically uncertain and catastrophic, but even now it looks as if creative writing has done noticeably better than most. There is good reason therefore to view any bright-line distinction between creative and explanatory work as incompatible with our student's interests and our own priorities. I have attempted to show here that it is also not in line with our practice. Explanation and expression are tied in the bond of knowing. The relative success of creative writing in the otherwise beleaguered market for the humanities is an occasion to make the most of this. Once again, I don't want us to change what we do. I want to change how we understand what we do. The fact of medium coincidence means that we are never far from the materials we write about. As we say all the time, we get closer to them the more we try to understand or convey understanding of them. Let us then praise the artfulness of remaining close, of quotation and imitation and summary. And let us extend that praise to the possible forms that closeness might take, when we assign papers to students, evaluate each other's work, and observe, as we are at present, new genres of critical writing emerging in our midst. Criticism is a form of creative writing in the full sense of the term. In the next chapter, I'll take up how we recognize and validate what is true (or not) in a work of criticism. One implication of the present discussion is that verification of this kind is among other things an aesthetic judgment.

Verification

No one writing criticism feels like they are just making stuff up. I don't have a survey to support the claim, but my guess would be that most believe they are getting at truth and so contributing to a project of knowledge. But how do we judge whether a work of criticism has succeeded at that goal or achieved that end? I have maintained over the course of this book that judgments of this kind turn on such criteria as whether a reading is apt or the material has been gotten right. These are evaluative criteria and open to charges of circularity or bias. I have aimed therefore to define "apt" and "right" as far as I can with respect to special practices of quotation, imitative elaboration, and summary while recognizing that these do not comprise the whole of either close reading or critical practice. The present chapter will turn to acts and institutions of verification. It will ask how the discipline of literary studies validates work done in the field, if it does so at all. There ought to be a relation between method and verification, as there is in other fields, so what is it?

I have written in earlier chapters of the importance of what Gilbert Ryle calls "appraisal" in the evaluation of skill. The idea is that it is crucial for acts of skill to be recognized by a group or population who has the experience and wherewithal to judge whether someone has gotten it right or is good at what they aim to achieve. Depending upon the sphere of life, the relevant group might be other practitioners of a craft or connoisseurs of the arts or trained experts in a field. Recognition of this kind is necessary for skill to be a skill because no practice happens on its own, absent a framework of training, support, judgment, care, praise, revision, or rebuke. In the academy, this framework exists in disciplines of teaching and research whose task it is to understand some part of the world.[1] Here the appraisal of the work also acts as or toward a verification of the work, a judgment that it gets at some truth and helps us know something. This kind of judgment will be most familiar and fraught in the sciences, where it is connected, as I will discuss below, to practices of replication and abstraction. Yet there is an analogous if distinct set of practices in the humanities as well, in which to appraise a work of criticism is to say that it has gotten something right about the world it endeavors to understand. There the humanistic disciplines in all their instances of recognition and peer review do their own version of what the sciences do. They credit a dexterous and adroit engagement with the encountered world.

For some, this kind of argument might bear a faint resemblance to a cluster of older positions put forward most notably by Stanley Fish on the role of "interpretive communities" in setting the range and suitability of readings in literary studies. I want to emphasize now that this is not the case, and that institutions of appraisal operate quite differently from how Fish understood them to. The difference is instructive. Fish argued that any verdict about whether an interpretation is right, wrong, or even plausible will be made "by those who write and judge articles of publication in learned journals, by those who read and listen to papers at professional meetings, by those who seek and award tenure in innumerable departments of English and comparative literature, by the armies of graduate students for whom knowledge of the rules is a real mark of professional initiation."[2] One could go on, but the list is not wholly inaccurate. What's inaccurate is the epistemology. On Fish's view, these communities are themselves the only limit placed upon interpretation. "The text is always a function of interpretation" because interpretation is always in the business of "producing the text" according to widely held rules of the game (342). The authority of any given interpretation thus resides within the sphere of interpreters itself without constraint from the rest of the world.

There is room in this account for craft, for skill, and for getting it right only to the extent to which they refer back to the interpretive community. You get the rules right or are skilled at getting your interpretation credited over someone else's. That's it. The argument was made in the service of a kind of anti-foundationalism common at the time, one skeptical about the ability or even desire for intellectual work to get a proper handle on the world. The present study shares none of this view. I don't think it gives an accurate account of the actual practices of criticism, which as we have seen have the properties they do because they reach out to and make something from what they analyze. I also don't think it gives an attractive account. Why would we want to view criticism as epistemically inert, now at a moment when it is so easy to get rid of entirely? The contrast is important, however, because it points to the fact of constraint in the world itself, not just in the community interpreting the world.[3] Once more, the world pushes back. Here the difference is large. Fish and others of the moment were right to draw out the role played by institutions of evaluation and appraisal. Skilled action does not occur on its own, but rather within contexts and standards it also modifies. The very nature of the skill, however,

lies in its relation to what is given, whether that is thread, nema-
todes, or sonnets. Fish and others were mistaken to refer skill back
only to the community and its "presently recognized interpretive
strategies for producing the text" (347). The cost of this mistake—
happily incurred though now deeply regretted—was not having
any account of claims verified or knowledge made in the practice
of criticism.[4]

For method to be method, it ought to make some part of the
world intelligible, not twist it to its will. Once again, the difference
of view here is instructive. To understand the world is to grapple
with its constraints, yet these may be broken (for example) by
straining quoted language against the words and worlds in which
it is encased. On such occasions, the intended effect is less getting
it right, in the sense I have defined it, than having words seem to
say something other than what one thinks they should say, a certain
magnetism of critical mastery. So, for example, when Fish wants
to argue that Milton's *Samson Agonistes* stages the defeat of singular interpretations by having its titular hero become "a surface with
no essence," he presents Samson turning into a version of Delilah:
"The result of having thus 'divulg'd the secret gift of God / To a de-
ceitful Woman' is, he is sure, to be 'sung and proverb'd for a Fool';
and what is worse, as one so 'proverb'd,' he has been reduced to
the condition of being a 'scorn and gaze.'"[5] Here the quotations
add to each other as they progress, spilling into a second independent clause barely contained by the semicolon. Milton's "rig-
orously worked-out logic" finds an echo in the critic, who makes
the short-form agreement between parts of speech inside and outside of quotation marks sit in deliberate abrasion with the larger pile
from which the quoted material is taken (467). Samson becomes a
"kind of billboard, successively and passively receiving the imprint

of someone else's meaning" (468). Or rather, *Samson* has become
a kind of billboard, as rigor amounts less to working within than to
overcoming the limits of what is given via a familiar if strenuously
executed allegory of interpretation: the drama of a critic imprint-
ing his meaning on the world and convincing the community to go
along with his reading.

That drama may be dazzling, but it loses the creativity and
knowledge work of stitching words to words already in a pattern. I
want to be clear about this. I have referred on occasion here to the
virtuosity of written criticism. By virtuosity, however, I do not mean
spectacles of unusual performance that hold us in awe. I mean literary criticism as it practiced all the time, everywhere, as part of
the ordinary science and everyday brilliance of the discipline itself.
I mean the kind of thing you find when you pick up any journal of
criticism and pass your eyes over an article of interest. Pause to look
under the hood, and you notice that the everyday life of writing in
literary studies puts in motion a suite of highly skilled practices in
its manner of quotation and deixis, imitated speech and summary.
We take these practices for granted only because after a time they
become instinctive and pass unnoticed. Drawing them out provides
a glimpse of the epistemic infrastructure of literary analysis, the
unremarked-upon methods that guide more visible acts of interpretation. Every discipline has a suite of such practices, just as every discipline verifies that these practices have been done well and
so justifies their claims to create knowledge. That close reading is
in actual fact a practice of writing, not so much intensive reflection
and rumination as intensive finesse and dexterity, has special importance in this context. Writing or some other external form is the
only venue in which ideas may in fact appear so as to be verified. In
this respect, the appraisal of any "reading" is less of the ideas them-

selves, if such a thing could be said to exist, than the enactment of ideas in practice. That is what gets appraised and so confirmed or disproven. One should of course think hard as one reads, but "reading" as method doesn't start until one writes because it is writing that does or does not get a proper handle on the world, or at least that part with which it shares a medium.

*   *   *

I have wanted to consider the epistemology of literary criticism in a way that might reclaim truth for the practice without holding it to standards of proof hostile or ill-suited to the enterprise itself. Let us banish the specter of positivism from our commitment to the epistemic. Asking whether a reading is true is just another way of asking whether the critic has applied her "special criteria" to her "special tasks" and so "gotten it right." This is neither to lower the stakes on method nor to give criticism a pass on evidence. It is instead to get a preliminary sense of how the skilled practice of critical writing makes and supports truth claims, as does the skilled practice of any other discipline of knowledge. It is to get a sense, in other words, of what verification aims to confirm and how verification works in practice. If, in the case of criticism, the truth or falsity of a given assertion is inseparable from how well the assertion is made, how well the assertion is made is inseparable from how well its objects are handled. By considering verification in this manner, we may reconcile our intuitive sense that testing a given reading by holding it to facts—"falsifying it"—seems opposed to the way arguments in the field proceed with our equally intuitive sense that readings are or ought to be responsible to the features of texts and world they endeavor to explain. Nothing invalidates a piece of criticism more than its breaking the fine composition of what is read, either by the force of error or the weight of brackets, ellipses, and interpolation. All the same, the facts of a given reading cannot be separated from the apt performance of that reading: "mark" is a matter of being because the pronoun and verb fit "mark the mark on me too" just so; "preserv'd" and "restor'd" are ambivalent because the conditional includes them and so on. There is no need to place "it is true that" before the rest of a sentence of criticism because the truth claim is implicit and embodied in the virtuosity of the sentence itself. The words fit the explanandum, or they don't.

This criterion of fit is specific to medium and applies across the various procedures of quotation, imitative extension, and summary I have discussed. Fit entails that every act of criticism is as unique as the sentences from which it is made, each a singular composite of two orders of writing. This uniqueness creates an important difference between verification in the literary humanities and in other disciplines of knowledge. One non-negotiable demand of scientific practice, for example, is that its findings are replicable.[6] Get an interesting result, and the experiment should be run again, by oneself or someone else. Successful duplication is essential to demonstrating that the matter has been gotten right. In fact, the sciences have been thrown into some disarray over the past decade by a widespread failure of notable studies to be replicated. This so-called "replication crisis" began in psychology and then spread to nearby disciplines in the social and natural sciences.[7] The history is now well-known, and I don't intend to go over it except to say that it brought back into discussion norms of scientific procedure that had long been taken for granted. Thus the opening paragraph of a recent survey of the crisis in the field-leading journal *Behavioral and Brain Sciences*:

The ability to systematically replicate research findings is a fundamental feature of the scientific process. Indeed, the idea that observations can be recreated and verified by independent sources is usually seen as a bright line of demarcation that separates science from non-science. A defining feature of science is that researchers do not merely accept claims without being able to critically evaluate the evidence for them. Independent replication of research findings is an essential step in this evaluation process, and, thus, replication studies should play a central role in science and in efforts to improve scientific practices.[8]

The impersonal tone of the sentences mimics the theoretical content. Science needs to be detached from any one experiment, with its singular point of view or unexamined motive, and secured to a plenum of experiments that then verify or discredit findings. In the influential terms of Karl Popper alluded to here, replication of this kind "demarcates" science from non-science.[9] All of this should go without saying, the authors suggest, and yet things have gotten to the point that the principle needs to be drawn out from the woodwork of method. Scientific knowledge is distinct from individual accidents of the practice. It is abstractable and may be reworded.

Things are markedly different for criticism. Do a reading the same way again to make sure that it yields the same result, and you will appear to be losing your mind. Repeat the performance of someone else, and you will be guilty of plagiarism. To argue, as I have, that literary criticism has a method that aims at truth just as the sciences do is (again) not to argue that it has the same method as the sciences or the same understanding of its method. Replication is important to science because, ideally understood, its results ought to be the same from any and every point of view. They ought to be objective in that sense. By comparison, critical results consist in one view held in a kind of braided tension with another, one's own words and words already made. Verification in literary criticism doesn't happen in the impossible or absurd practice of doing a reading again because there is no result independent of perspective that could be replicated. So how does it happen at all?

I closed the last chapter with the claim that criticism is a form of creative writing and the evaluation of critical prose a kind of aesthetic judgment. I meant to draw attention to the way that criticism makes sentences from sentences and to set up the idea that the evaluation of critical argument concerns how well that making is done.[10] I'd like to expand on this now, as a way of understanding aptness in criticism as the loose equivalent to replication in science, each a criterion to validate work in a manner appropriate to its domain. As an evaluative term, "apt" sits nicely beside terms like "adroit," "agile," and "dexterous" because it describes an almost or sometimes physical craftwork in the act of knowing. The word itself comes from *aptus*, for fitted, the Latin past participle of *apere*, to fasten or attach.[11] Knowledge is apt when it derives from a linking of the knower to the world. Sentences with embedded quotations demonstrate this vividly because the fastening works along the joints of syntax, but the same is the case for the looser fittings of deixis, imitative extension, and summary. Each one is an attachment specific to language, as mitering is to wood or battement to dance. When any one of them is appraised, the judgment concerns the attachment's quality, its elegance or perspicuity of shape, its mastery of the medium at hand. None is a mute contemplation of a finished form, and each commingles with a world that is in reach. As an appraisal of quality, therefore, the judgment of criticism is at one and the same time of craft aesthetics and craft epistemology. It evaluates a creative attachment to the given, an attachment to what I've described as a literary ecology: words in the intimate surround.

Some features of the aesthetic dimension to this judgment will help to situate consensus as well as disagreement in the appraisal of truth claims. First of all, validation is not a singular activity, but spread across the range of institutions and practices that constitute the structure of peer review. In this respect at least, the emphasis on interpretive community, if we want to call it that, is on the right track. Any judgment is multiauthored and instanced, something passed on from one moment of a process to another. Of equal and related importance, any personal act of critical judgment takes as its origin and outcome this same community, this public. In this context, we might consult no less an authority than Immanuel Kant. "Whenever we make a judgment declaring something to be beautiful, we permit no one to hold a different opinion, even though we base our judgment only on our feeling rather than on concepts: hence we regard this underlying feeling as a common rather than as a private feeling."[12] Following on Kant, let us say that when we recognize a piece of critical writing as apt and to have gotten something right, we bring the public of academic criticism into existence as an imaginary partner. We presume that the recognition is held by others. Any singular act of judgment, of course, admits of dissensus. It is normative not descriptive; "it does not say that everyone *will* agree with my judgment, but that he *ought* to" (89). And yet for that reason, the act requires and carries along with it a group to whom "ought" applies and from where "ought" begins. Strange as it may seem, to state that a certain summary of plot or writing in the manner of an author fits is to state that it is beautiful and then to imagine that everyone agrees.

The judging and so validating of works of criticism is in this way a social activity, even in its most solitary instances. It always presumes the existence of others with whom one shares a vocation, outlook, feeling, training, and skill. Everyone ought to agree with everyone else's judgment of another's work because we draw from this common endeavor and possess the same intuitions. The aesthetic judgment of criticism thus momentarily suspends differences in rank, privilege, and security.[13] It has a quasi-utopian, quasi-hey-go-along-with-me-for-a-moment structure of address. Kant believed that judgments of this kind are subjective because they are based on feeling instead of concepts and because they are relatively separate from identifying properties of the object. Members of an interpretive community, on this view, share a set of intuitions more than they follow the same rules or point at the same things. The personal yet common nature of aesthetic judgment as Kant describes it, therefore, might go some distance in describing how verification operates without replication in the literary humanities. To strip the evaluation of its intuitive basis would be to deprive it of its very nature; to call it mere bias would be to miss its public grounds.

All the same, I want to stick with the idea that judgments of this variety are not subjective according to Kant's or anyone else's sense of the term. In its multipart and staged structure, of course, peer review has a design that extends beyond a single person. It is not "subjective" as that term circulates in more informal speech as a synonym for partial, surely an important fact for the notion that aesthetic judgment presumes consensus. But the critical view and its appraisal aren't subjective in Kant's more ontological sense either. When Kant argues that "a judgment of taste ... is merely *contemplative*, i.e., it is a judgment that is indifferent to the existence of the object," he means that we consider the "character of the object only by holding it up to our feeling of pleasure and displeasure" (51). We are not supposed to take an interest in what we are judging beyond the feeling that it raises in us. This seems short of the mark so far as the aesthetic dimension to evaluating criticism goes. Judgments of taste or considerations of beauty in literary criticism play a decisive role in establishing validity, but they refer all the time to the character of the object, its well-formedness and apt handling of language. That is because they concern the application and practice of craft, with its painstaking treatment of a world at hand. The act of evaluating this craft examines the composing and manipulation of words by those working in the same medium. In this respect, Kant seems perhaps less our guide than some of the British philosophers who preceded him, for whom delimiting what in their material properties made artworks beautiful, such as Francis Hutcheson's "unity in variety," or locating value in active making rather than contemplative viewing were often the goal.[14] For this way of thinking, indifference to works is impossible since one is always in the business of their creation or consideration. One is, for example, in the business of adding words to words so as to understand them, like the painter in Jonathan Richardson's 1725 account of portraiture who "must be a mechanic, his hand and eye ... as expert as his head is clear and lively."[15] Literary criticism's aesthetic practice is medium entanglement and so the terminology of subject and object inadequate for understanding and appraising the skill at hand.

In his famous study of craft aesthetics and epistemology, the furniture maker David Pye opens with a gambit: "Material in the raw is nothing much. Only worked material has quality." Scandalously for anyone with a taste for chairs and cabinetry, he brought out as his example that "English Walnut is not good material. Most of the tree is leaf mold and firewood. It is only because of workmanlike felling and converting and drying and selection and machining and setting out and cutting and fitting and assembly and finishing—particularly finishing—that a very small proportion of the tree comes to be thought of as good material."[16] The point of Pye's well-crafted polysyndeton was that the walnut we admire or sit on comes into being through dexterous "working" and the accomplished use of tools. Seen this way, the interest a craftsperson takes in her materials concerns how to turn them from one thing to another and in the process how to apprehend what makes them what they are. The woodworker brings the beautiful walnut to existence as she comes to understand it better, not in the way that a botanist would but as someone who touches and manipulates their medium. I have argued that criticism ought to be understood as a similarly immersive practice. For my present purposes, that means its evaluation is something other than contemplative. Like the evaluation of woodwork, the evaluation of criticism is a consideration of "worked material" by those who are able to put their hands in the place of the artisan and so judge whether one set of sentences fits with another (or not).

Judgment of this kind happens in the process of verification, as important in the humanities as the sciences. In neither domain is there some final, extra-institutional test that would sort the sound from the specious. All that we have are the fallible organizations and procedures that constitute review by peers, and all we can do is monitor that these organizations and procedures work well.[17] The response to the crisis in replication that has beset the sciences might in this respect serve as a model for the humanities: a several-fold and ongoing inspection of method as it breaks down by field.[18] Once again, the lesson is not that the humanities ought to take on the methods of other disciplines. Quite the contrary, the replication crisis underscores that method varies by discipline, the constant theme of this book, and does so because the encountered and studied world itself varies. The lesson, therefore, is that the humanities, like the sciences, ought to consider what makes their methods methodical, how truth claims are built, supported, and verified. The replication crisis has brought out often tacit assumptions and practices about what it means to "replicate" work in the first place, about, for example, whether it means to do an experiment again or to make your data and code available for inspection. Something like that is due in the humanities. For the literary disciplines, the corresponding effort would be to consider how we find work to be reliable, impressive, and credible. It would be to look into the practices of writing criticism at their several stages from close reading to contextual elaboration to argumentative synthesis. I have spent time on dimensions of the first and have aspired to get to their most granular or micro-levels, emphasizing as well that similar light can and ought to be shined on other dimensions to our methods at different scales of analysis. The problem of verification emerges when we consider appraisal as a process that accompanies and gives credence to all of this. Has the work gotten it right? Is the reading adroit, elegant, and dexterous? I have argued that such matters of epistemic and aesthetic judgment take consensus as their aspirational premise, but in such a way that recognizes disagreement, compromise, and error as inevitable and acceptable.[19] That is only a beginning. The humanities have not faced an event like the replication crisis in part because they never had the authority that the natural sciences do, no perch of methodological scrupulousness from which to fall. Our crises are, in this respect, at once more long-standing and more urgent. To address them, we need to spend more time on what validates work in the field and therefore gives authority to the discipline as one of knowledge, now at a time of extreme peril.

* * *

Verification is important because the work it supports tells us something that we would lose were it shoddy or were the enterprise itself to shut down. Let us then be clear. Sentences that embed, point to, extend, or summarize other sentences and their parts are right (or wrong) according to how well the words or clauses fit individual dimensions of the world. When I have used the term "world" in formulations like this, I of course have meant language, the only kind of thing one could embed or extend in a sentence. What is gotten right in this respect are usually works of literature, however we may choose to define the term. That is surely the main share of what it means for criticism to tell the truth and surely the main criterion for verifying and validating any particular work of critical writing. To the degree to which criticism tells truths about the world of which literature is one part—a world studied by other disciplines as well—it is because literature has its own method, its own way of arranging the topics it would engage. Literature may only be one part of the world, but it interacts with the rest. For this reason, critics habitually find themselves taking up matters of interest to those working in other fields. To list them would be to do an inventory of all the topics of plausible concern for criticism. That would likely be less useful than understanding the procedure that moves from practices of quotation or imitative extension or summary to truth claims shareable with a scholar from another field. I have described this process as inescapably creative, a making of novel artifacts from the medium in which literature itself is made.

I would add as a last word that such creativity extends to whatever literature itself engages, that criticism is in this respect a kind of world making. To understand how this is so—how a "reading" of a poem on, for example, the topic of harvesting apples might be of interest for a scholar working on sustainable agriculture—would be to provide the ground for ongoing conversations and collaboration among disciplines. But we can't have that without recognizing that we tell the truth.

Public Criticism for a Public Humanities

I have attempted to describe an intellectual practice located in the institutions of higher education: in colleges and universities; peer-reviewed journals and university presses; in conferences, lectures, and symposia. My account is of one academic endeavor among others, each involved in the effort to explain and so transform the world. Recent years have witnessed a flowering of academic criticism written outside these particular institutions or at the nexus between them and a wider readership, in venues such as the *Los Angeles Review of Books*, *n+1*, *Public Books*, *Lit Hub*, and so on. The vitality of such public-facing criticism has a clear relation to the present crisis in higher education. It means to develop an audience and support for the humanities at a time when majors are dropping and humanistic writing is ignored or misunderstood. It means to find work and an audience for scholars marooned by the present employment catastrophe. What does this new institutional ground mean for method and morale in the field at large? There are no easy answers. My thoughts here are speculative, in part because the history is so ongoing and in part because I think it best to remain at once upbeat and open-ended. One challenge of public-facing writing is that it has yet no clear feedback into more traditional academic practice. The route from the prose to its audience is in one direction. Beneath this challenge lies the worrisome gap between those with stable employment in universities and younger scholars set to contest and enliven the field. A route back to the academy would require a next generation to take up and so transform the practice. I close then with method and its institutions at a moment of real flux.

The term "public humanities" covers a range of activities and initiatives, from curatorial projects to lectures to art making and beyond.[1] My interest here is not so much with the category itself as the adjacent desire that academics write for audiences outside of the university. This desire has been much in the air for the past decade and, like everything else after COVID, has accelerated with the sense that disciplines need to redefine their missions amid scarce resources, declining enrollments, and uncertain futures. For some the importance of public-facing writing is that it convinces people to support work done in universities. As Judith Butler puts it, writing as the president of the Modern Language Association, public-facing writing is a way to "make the case for what we do that appeals to those who already value literature and the imagination."[2] The pronoun in this sentence and others like it refers to established and relatively secure academics implored to modulate their address for civic engagement. Much of the recent interest in the public humanities in general, and public-facing criticism in particular, has taken on this understandable preoccupation with PR. Let us stop being so insular. People like literature. They just don't like literature *professors*. For others, the desire or demand for a public humanities expresses a sense that writing for fellow scholars is itself wanting in significance and impact. There the idea is not so much to translate private scholarship for a larger audience as to question the very idea of humanistic expertise. On this view, the "decline and crisis of the *academic* humanities at four-year college," as two less friendly analysts have phrased it, is "a very specific kind of crisis ... limited to one very particular kind of ecosystem," something "akin to the crisis for coal mining communities brought about by a switch to renewable energy sources."[3]

It is important to bear in mind the anti-intellectual use toward which the idea of a public humanities has been put by the corporate university among others, if only to encourage public-facing work within a broader effort to rebuild the liberal arts. Writing for the public, in Butler's words, demonstrates "the distinctive contribution that the humanities can make to all fields of knowledge by keeping alive fields of value that are irreducible to instrumentality and profitability."[4] The study of literature and the other arts keeps alive values of truth, justice, and beauty that support collective flourishing, and itself is kept alive by active research and training from one generation to the next. I have focused on research and training in the effort to provide a positive description of humanistic method, something lacking in recent defenses of the humanities. Much of the recent interest in public criticism, however, has emerged as a response to the sharply felt labor crisis and the sense that graduate education as currently structured cannot be sustained. Learning how to write for a public is not only better for our reputation, on this view; it might also lead to a wider variety of jobs for graduate students and the precariously employed. In this respect, the emphasis on public writing is part of a larger overhaul of the PhD so that it does more than prepare students for careers as tenure-track professors. Thus Leonard Cassuto and Robert Weisbuch write in a recent and influential call for graduate-program reform: "As public scholarship develops, its close relationship with career diversity emerges more and more clearly."⁵ A lot turns on the public turn. Let's take a look.

On its face, the largest difference between public-facing criticism and the ordinary writing of the discipline is simply one of platform: the online magazine or website in the first case; the academic journal or university press in the second. (Every one of the venues I listed above exists exclusively or predominantly online.) With this difference in platform comes significant differences in both access and procedure. Although public-facing criticism sometimes requires a modest subscription to read, it is ostensibly open to everyone with an internet connection. Traditional academic criticism in contrast lies on the other side of restrictive library access. Editors alone do the vetting for public-facing criticism. Editorial boards and peer reviewers vet academic articles and monographs. Public-facing criticism accordingly moves from conception to appearance at a faster speed and has the look at least of reaching more readers, while academic criticism contributes to the durée of scholarly discussion with the ballast and authority of already having been read.

These are ideal-typical contrasts whose concrete embodiments surely look somewhat different on the ground. My interest, however, is less with gauging whether and to what extent public venues reach more readers than more traditionally academic ones—an empirical matter and currently unknown in the details—than with the idea that they do and with the very real attraction this idea has for a discipline looking for renewal. In this context, I'd like to pursue two questions that will bring the concerns of this book to the pitched context of its writing. Is it right to speak of a criticism that deliberately eschews the academy as having a method? And what is the relation between the desire for public criticism and the discipline's acute labor crisis? The two questions are more deeply related than one might think at first glance. Answering them will help us understand the practice and rationale of academically informed criticism written for a non-academic audience at this moment of intense hope and intense worry.

Public-facing criticism has a method because it is in the game of knowledge. In fact, one of the promises of public criticism is that it brings academic knowledge to a larger audience by performing its method with a modulated voice on a different platform.[6] The emphasis falls of course on clarity, on shucking the idiomatic particularity and grammatical subordination that marks academic style across the disciplines. In this respect, public criticism takes on the stylistic preferences of the broader sphere of journalism. An equal emphasis falls on political or social topicality or simply current events, so that works that seem difficult to understand or from a different age reveal themselves to be relevant for any number of contemporary readers. The promise is in this way to bring scholarly expertise to bear on matters of widespread concern. At the same time, and in reverse direction, public criticism can have an essayistic, first-person address typically lacking in ordinary academic prose, with comparisons drawn between characters and events in literary texts and the experience of the critic herself.[7] Beneath these distinguishing emphases in style and subject matter, public criticism shares the baseline skill and know-how of its academic parent. The method just travels from one platform to another so that it might scale up and face out in a different guise.

Rather than discuss method in the abstract, however, let us once again look at method in action. In a recent essay in *Public Books*, Margaret Ronda begins with a question. Given climate change and social crisis, she asks, "How can poetry call attention to creative modes of survival and persistence, human and nonhuman?" She wants to draw her reader's interest to new collections of poems that seem urgent to read and think with at this perilous moment of planetary history. Valerie Martínez's *Count*, for example, entwines enumeration with mattering, asking us, as it were, to count what counts. Ronda's sentences in turn encourage us to linger with the poet's noticing. "Martínez describes dreams of 'stick figures / in a giant earth tome' of catastrophes: 'book of mudslides,' 'book of super-storms,' 'book of drought-devastated fields.'"[8] Note the performance again. Ronda glides the embedded phrase into her preposition so that the poem becomes the earth's library, issuing in sequential anaphora. This is the skilled practice of the critic's unseen labor, enabling her reader to look and to see poetry's transfiguration of the world into language that counts all living things. So, too, is the interpretive plot summary that allows Elissa Myers, in an essay in the *Los Angeles Review of Books*, to connect the heroine of Charlotte Brontë's *Villette* to herself along the axis of shared obsessive-compulsive disorder. Myers deftly retells the story so it contains "clues through which I came to recognize, in Lucy, myself," and so its pivotal reveal at the midpoint of the narrative discloses truths about not just the character but the reader and their shared condition. "After teaching at the pensionnat for months, Lucy suddenly finds herself alone during a long vacation. Her thoughts seem to 'intrude' on her, miserably from elsewhere. She has bad dreams as well as what seem to be waking nightmares, and struggles to account for a 'nameless experience that had the hue, the mien, the terror of a visitation from eternity.'" In this well-crafted mini-narrative, Myers pins words from the novel at the end of her own in such a way that the synopsis comes around to an experience at once private and common: "an intensity of suffering, and a painful feeling that both faith and language had deserted me."[9] Moving in the other direction, finally,

Omari Weekes's *Bookforum* piece on Colson Whitehead's *Harlem Shuffle* transitions from the 1964 World Fair's "slick wonderland of Googie architecture and Picturephones" to a twenty-first century "placated by individual success rather than racial uplift." The move works on a silent removal of the marks of quotation that has the critic speak to the reader in the voice of the author: "'He was a wall between the criminal world and the straight world, necessary, bearing the load.' Carrying that weight is how Carney survives." Without altering tense or tone, Weekes scales from the voice and dialogue of the novel to the moment in which the novel is composed, read, and discussed. His prose moves up from the imagined mid-century and faces out to a present that includes the critic, his audience, and the "unfulfilled" promise of the civil rights movement.[10]

The mission statement of *Public Books* declares that "experts who devote their lives to mastering their subjects need to be heard."[11] These examples and others like them remind us that we speak and listen in ways specific to expertise. There is a method to what is said and what is learned. In this way, public criticism is an unqualified good. Every time a critic is heard, someone learns something new about the corner of the world the critic finds of compelling interest. More of the world comes into view and is altered in the viewing. I have tried to show how this is in literal form a beautiful thing. Let us have more of it. Let us also bring to traditional venues more of the inventiveness that critics have found in modulating their voice for public consumption. To recognize the epistemic and creative value of criticism as it is actually written is not to block new styles in the field. Far from it. It is to welcome the power that comes from engaging one's audience, including those outside the academy.

Whether in idea or fact, this kind of synergy is well-suited for troubled times, a subsidy of vigor in a place of need. That is one reason public criticism has played a large role in recent efforts to reform the curriculum of graduate education. But it is not the only reason. Learning how to write for a public, many believe, will expand job prospects for PhDs in the literary humanities and therefore should be encouraged as one part of diversifying career training and outcomes. How are we to evaluate this important claim? On one level, it is unarguably true. Anything helps, and all new skills create different opportunities. Some measurable future for some younger scholars will come from making public criticism an option for graduate training. On another level, however, the claim can easily be misleading. Public-facing writing itself is a career available to the very few. The work is piecemeal and poorly remunerated (in the venues I've listed, about $100 to $300 an article). Salaried positions in the proximate fields of journalism and publishing are subject to the same economic pressures as the academy and have their own pathways and modes of credentialization. There is finally nothing for public criticism like the system-wide infrastructure of employment and reproduction of the labor supply that lies beneath and has built criticism as we know it. In its place, in fact, is a mixture of patronage, connections, and elite bias that in certain ways echoes the old-boy network in its most extreme forms. "Adjacency to *The New Yorker*," as one English professor describes the new model of prestige, already exists for some more than others.[12] It would be a sad irony if, in the effort to encourage new voices and open new possibilities, the discipline placed its hopes in corridors easiest to tread by those with the most privilege. By pointing all of this out, I do not mean to discourage us from making public criticism a core part of the English PhD. I mean to make sure it serves as many as possible and to keep us from using it as an alibi for not solving the employment crisis as best we can.

No amount of curricular reform will fix the human costs of the employment crisis; only structural reform can do that. No amount will fix the epistemic costs either. Those costs are equally steep. I began this book by arguing that disciplines survive by moving scholars up the ranks, that younger voices keep inquiry alive by challenging what they have been taught. Absent this counterflow of ideas, disciplines harden into a clergy of the never changing. Consider in this light again the mission statement of *Public Books*. "It is desirable," the editors write, "for academics to speak to a broader audience, and exciting for readers outside of the academy to debate what scholars have to say."[13] Each side of this statement is true, and together they make a good case for public criticism. But note the direction of address. There is no feedback from the audience to the scholars, nor could there be, because the audience of public criticism is not imagined to write. Their debate is not in the same medium nor on the same platform as the critics. The speech and the debate don't have the archival persistence and citational evolution of scholarly argument. Don't get me wrong. Public criticism can and ought to derive all sorts of energizing ideas from the communities it addresses. That is one of the things that makes it an unambiguous gain for the discipline. But it won't keep the discipline alive without jobs for its young. It won't do so because it doesn't contribute to the ongoing, medium-specific continuation and transformation of inquiry. For that we need writing that responds to what has come before it, incorporated into and sustaining the life cycle of literary criticism. And for that we need, and need to fight for, abundant and well-paid human labor.

Public criticism is a good in itself, not the savior of the literary humanities nor a substitute for creating full-time, ideally tenure-track, jobs. It is one example of the value of the humanities for social flourishing and of criticism for understanding the world. Keeping it alive, however, requires the same commitment to humanistic inquiry that would sustain the academic disciplines. That commitment has been eroded by a many-pronged catastrophe whose constituents hardly need to be enumerated: a drop-off in enrollments; an over-emphasis on STEM; an instrumentalist view of learning; a steady and steep decline in funding; the corporatization of higher education, including a widespread turn to casual labor. As a whole, the humanities can provide a language for understanding and resisting this catastrophe, but not without a belief in their worth. Enrollments and funding and employment won't return if the practitioners of humanistic learning don't believe in and advocate for what they study and teach. Among other urgent tasks, we need to believe in and advocate for the methods we use when we write about literature. They are at the heart of our claim to tell the truth and to create knowledge worth having.

Acknowledgments

Criticism and Truth began as an essay in *Critical Inquiry*. I thank the editors for their reading and for permission to reprint the sentences that had appeared first in their pages. It builds on a defense of disciplinary thinking and analyses of the academic job market I have published from time to time in the *Chronicle of Higher Education*. The spirit and several stray formulations of the *Chronicle* articles make their way here, and I thank Len Gutkin especially for this conversation throughout. See "Criticism and Truth," *Critical Inquiry* 47, no. 2 (Winter 2021): 418–40; and "The Humanities after Covid-19," in *Chronicle Review*, July 23, 2020.

Alan Thomas encouraged me to continue writing about literary criticism and epistemology, and Nan Da and Anahid Nersessian were excited when he brought the idea of a short book to them. These pages wouldn't exist without them.

The ideas and reading for the original essay began in a class on literary theory I taught with Marta Figlerowicz. Marta, John Durham Peters, and Caleb Smith read and commented on the essay at various stages of its growth into a book. My graduate student summer reading group discussed recent criticism with me in the sun and provided invaluable feedback on the section on public criticism. I am grateful for the conversation and commentary from audiences at the City College of New York, Cornell University, the University of California, Berkeley and Irvine campuses, the University of Rhode Island, Warsaw University, Yale University, and York University, UK.

This book is a celebration of academic practice and academic life written in the hope that both can remain open to the scholars of the future. It is dedicated to my father, Isaac Kramnick, whose memory is a blessing and whose practice an ideal.

Notes

Introduction

1. See John Guillory, *Cultural Capital: The Problem of Literary Canon Formation* (Chicago: University of Chicago Press, 1993).

2. For the numbers, see Jonathan Kramnick, "The Humanities after Covid-19," *Chronicle of Higher Education*, July 23, 2020.

3. Tim Ingold, *Perceiving the Environment: Essays on Livelihood, Dwelling and Skill* (London: Routledge, 2000), 353; subsequent citations are made parenthetically.

4. Tim Ingold, "Five Questions of Skill," *Cultural Geographies* 25, no. 1 (2018): 159.

5. See Ernest Sosa, *A Virtue Epistemology*, vol. 1 of *Apt Belief and Reflective Knowledge*, 2 vols. (Oxford: Oxford University Press, 2007), 29 passim.

6. See Jonathan Kramnick and Anahid Nersessian, "Form and Explanation," *Critical Inquiry* 43, no. 3 (2017): 650–69.

7. See Jonathan Kramnick, *Paper Minds: Literature and the Ecology of Consciousness* (Chicago: University of Chicago Press, 2018).

Chapter One

1. We might say that the "method wars" began in 2009 with the special issue and introductory essay on "surface reading" and came to a soft close with the collection *Critique and Postcritique* cited below. This periodization would place the apex of method talk within the duration of the Obama administration, which seems about right.

2. Rita Felski, "Introduction," *New Literary History* 45 (Spring 2014): v.

3. Ibid.

4. Elizabeth S. Anker and Rita Felski, "Introduction," in *Critique and Post-critique*, ed. Anker and Felski (Durham, NC: Duke University Press, 2017), 1. In Felski's book-length treatment, the target is sometimes "mood and method" and sometimes just "mood" alone. Rita Felski, *The Limits of Critique* (Chicago: University of Chicago Press, 2015), 1.

5. David Kurnick, "A Few Lies: Queer Theory and Our Method Melodramas," *English Literary History* 87 (Summer 2020): 351. Kurnick refers here to the familiar roster of essays on reparative, surface, and anti-suspicious reading by Rita Felski, Eve Sedgwick, Steven Best and Sharon Marcus, and Heather Love.

6. Alasdair MacIntyre, *After Virtue*, 3rd ed. (1981; Notre Dame, IN: Notre Dame University Press, 2007), 187; subsequent citations are to this edition and are made parenthetically.

7. Rachel Sagner Buurma and Laura Heffernan, *The Teaching Archive: A New History for Literary Study* (Chicago: University of Chicago Press, 2021), 10, 11; subsequent citations are made parenthetically.

8. Eric Havelock, *The Muse Learns to Write: Reflections on Orality and Literacy from Antiquity to the Present* (New Haven, CT: Yale University Press, 1984), 55.

9. Andrew Piper, *Enumerations: Data and Literary Study* (Chicago: University of Chicago Press, 2018), 7; subsequent citations are made parenthetically.

10. For more on the hermeneutic circle, see my discussion in chapter 4.

11. On the desire for replication, see Andrew Piper and Matt Erlin, "Humanities: Let the Hypothesis Testing Begin," *Public Books*, October 21, 2021, https://www.publicbooks.org/humanities-let-the-hypothesis-testing-begin/.

12. Simon Blackburn, *On Truth* (New York: Oxford University Press, 2018), 72.

13. See, for example, Hoyt Long and Richard Jean So, "Literary Pattern Recognition: Modernism between Close Reading and Machine Learning," *Critical Inquiry* 42 (2016): 235–67.

14. See Jonathan Kramnick, "Against Literary Darwinism," *Critical Inquiry* 37 (Winter 2011): 315–47; Kramnick, "Literary Studies and Science: A Reply to My Critics," *Critical Inquiry* 38 (Winter 2012): 431–60; Kramnick, *Paper Minds*, 17–36; Kramnick and Anahid Nersessian, "Form and Explanation," 650–69; and Kramnick and Nersessian, "Forms and Explanations: A Reply to Our Critics," *Critical Inquiry* 44 (Autumn 2017): 164–74.

15. Michael Friedman, "Explanation and Scientific Understanding," *Journal of Philosophy* 71, no. 1 (1974): 13.

16. This much at least was the message of, among others, Paul Feyerabend's famous polemic, *Against Method* (London: Verso, 1975).

Chapter Two

1. On this point, I have benefited from discussions with Caleb Smith. For his argument that the metaphorical description of literary-critical practice as reading has allowed for interpretive positions to present themselves as ethical positions, see Caleb Smith, "Disciplines of Attention in a Secular Age," *Critical Inquiry* 45 (Summer 2019): 884–909.

2. There the practice is oral rather than written, but once again is externalized, something spoken out in collective, dialogic manner, with procedures of quotation and deixis more akin to the writing practice we call close reading than to contemplative reading with attention.

3. Stanislas Dehaene, *Reading in the Brain: The Science and Evolution of a Human Invention* (New York: Penguin, 2009), 1–2. The cognitive science of writing (which would include that of reading) is immediately relevant to the practice of literary study. See, for example, Ronald Kellogg, "Training Writing Skills: A Cognitive Developmental Perspective," *Journal of Writing Research* 1, no. 1 (2008): 1–26. Writing, on Kellogg's view, coordinates language, memory, thinking, and motor skills in a manner similar to playing music or chess and is similarly a trained skill realized in performance. See also 000n5 below.

4. Andrew Goldstone, "Close Reading as Genre," *Arcade: Literature, Humanities, and the World*, Stanford Humanities Center, arcade.stanford.edu/blogs/close-reading-genre.

5. John Guillory, "Close Reading: Prologue and Epilogue," *ADE Bulletin* 149 (2010): 11.

6. Jonathan Culler, "The Closeness of Close Reading," *ADE Bulletin* 149 (2010): 20.

7. Barbara Herrnstein Smith, "What Was 'Close Reading'?: A Century of Method in Literary Studies," *Minnesota Review* 87 (2016): 58.

8. Toril Moi, *Revolution of the Ordinary: Literary Studies after Wittgenstein, Austin, and Cavell* (Chicago: University of Chicago Press, 2017), 178.

9. Heather Love, "Close Reading and Thin Description," *Public Culture* 43, no. 3 (2013): 413.

10. Natalie Phillips, "Literary Neuroscience and History of Mind: An Interdisciplinary fMRI study of Attention and Jane Austen," in *The Oxford Handbook of Cognitive Literary Studies*, ed. Lisa Zunshine (Oxford: Oxford University Press, 2015), 59. Phillips's definition is particularly interesting because it is in the service of an interdisciplinary approach. Attentive focus is what we bring to other disciplines.

11. Elaine Auyoung, "What We Mean by Reading," *New Literary History* 51 (Winter 2020): 94.

12. This practice is sometimes called in-line quotation because quoted language remains within the line of printed text, rather than as a block with inset margins and without quotation marks. I prefer in-sentence quotation because the term emphasizes the syntactic and semantic unit rather than the layout of the page. In-sentence quotation gets a better handle on method, I think, because it emphasizes the relation among form, meaning, and truth whereas in-line quotation emphasizes appearance. Not all in-sentence quotations appear entirely in line (as will become apparent in my examples), nor are all quotations placed out of the unit of one's own sentence printed in block. Indeed, the opposite term to in-sentence quotation is for these reasons better captured as between-sentence quotation than block quotation, even as the latter expression is inescapably part of our disciplinary usage.

13. Eric Hayot has a brief discussion in *Elements of Academic Style: Writing for the Humanities* (New York: Columbia University Press, 2014), 153–55, but it is meant as a guide to aspiring critics more than a reflection on method.

14. Mary A. Favret, *War at a Distance: Romanticism and the Making of Modern Wartime* (Princeton, NJ: Princeton University Press, 2010), 59; subsequent citations are made parenthetically.

15. For "why questions" as central to critical explanation, see Kramnick and Nersessian, "Form and Explanation."

16. Christina Sharpe, *In the Wake: On Blackness and Being* (Durham, NC: Duke University Press, 2016), 49; subsequent citations are made parenthetically. Sharpe's chapter combines embedded quotation and close reading with close looking at photography, drawing out and combining methods that correspond to each medium.

17. See Sharpe's argument concerning "the metaphor of the wake in the entirety of its meanings" (17).

18. Seeta Chaganti, *Strange Footing: Poetic Form and Dance in the Late Middle Ages* (Chicago: University of Chicago Press, 2018), 20.

19. Elisa Tamarkin, *Apropos of Something: A History of Irrelevance and Relevance* (Chicago: University of Chicago Press, 2022), 10.

20. For more on the use of the literary present in contemporary criticism, see Paul Saint-Amour, "The Literary Present," *ELH* 85, no. 3 (2018): 367–92.

21. Paul Alpers, *What Is Pastoral?* (Chicago: University of Chicago Press, 1996), 253; subsequent citations are made parenthetically.

22. Demonstrative deixis is arguably *the* block mode. Consider the ubiquity of "in this passage," "in these lines," "this stanza," etc. It also tends to distinguish block forms of between-sentence quotation from those formatted within the typical layout of a paragraph. The space and indentation seems to facilitate or call out for acts of pointing.

23. Timothy Yu, *Diasporic Poetics: Asian Writing in the United States, Canada, and Australia* (Oxford: Oxford University Press, 2021), 58; subsequent citations are made parenthetically.

24. To get it right in the sense that the narrator's third person sounds like the character's first person. See for a counterexample James Wood on Saul Bellow's "writing over his character" and so getting the first to third person wrong. Wood, *How Fiction Works* (New York: Picador, 2008), 35–36.

25. George Eliot, *Daniel Deronda* (1872), as quoted in Nicholas Dames, *The Physiology of the Novel: Reading, Neural Science, and the Form of Victorian Fiction* (Oxford: Oxford University Press, 2007), 159; subsequent citations to Dames and Eliot are made parenthetically.

26. Eric Hayot, *Humanist Reason: A History, an Argument, a Plan* (New York: Columbia University Press, 2021), 167, 170.

27. For more on anti-reductionism as the key for thinking about interdisciplinarity, see Kramnick, *Paper Minds*, 17–36.

28. See Gilbert Ryle, *The Concept of Mind* (1949; repr., Chicago: University of Chicago Press, 2000), 25–61; subsequent citations are made parenthetically. The "knowing *how* and knowing *that*" distinction maps imperfectly onto a precursor distinction between *technē* (craft, technique, or art) and *epistēmē* (knowledge) in ancient philosophy. One important difference is that "knowing *how*" is a form of knowledge, something not always clear in the case of *technē*. See, for example, Aristotle, *Nichomachean Ethics*, book 6, where *epistēmē* is a "judgment about things that are universal and necessary" and *technē* is a "reasoned state

of capacity to make." Aristotle, *Ethica Nicomachea*, in *The Basic Works of Aristotle*, trans. W. D. Ross, ed. Richard McKeon (New York: Modern Library, 1941), 1027, 1025.

Chapter Three

1. For a synoptic account of the know-how debates, see Carlotta Pavese, "Skill in Epistemology I: Skill and Knowledge" and "Skill in Epistemology II: Skill and Know How," *Philosophy Compass* 11, no. 11 (2016): 642-49, 650-60.

2. Michael Polanyi, *Personal Knowledge: Towards a Post-Critical Philosophy* (Chicago: University of Chicago Press, 1958), 54.

3. See, for example, Michael Polanyi, "The Logic of Tacit Inference" (1964), in *Knowing and Being: Essays by Michael Polanyi* (Chicago: University of Chicago Press, 1969), 138-58.

4. Interesting support for this view can be found in the cognitive science of writing. Ronald Kellogg describes what he calls professional writing expertise as a practice involving thinking, language, memory, and motor skills. See "Professional Writing Expertise," in *The Cambridge Handbook of Expertise and Expert Performance*, ed. K. Anders Ericsson, Neil Charness, Robert R. Hoffman, and Paul J. Feltovich (New York: Cambridge University Press, 2002), 389-402.

5. On the semantics of quotation in this respect, see Donald Davidson, "Quotation," in *Inquiries into Truth and Method* (Oxford: Oxford University Press, 2001), esp. 92.

6. Jason Stanley, *Know How* (Oxford: Oxford University Press, 2011), 35. For Stanley and the intellectualists, knowing how to do something—drive a car with a manual transmission, say, or embed two lines from an Auden poem into your sentence—is a subset of knowing that something is the case because versions of such know-how answer an implicit question of the order "What is the way to drive a stick shift?" or "How do you wrap words around 'Far off like floating seeds the ships / Diverge on urgent voluntary errands' without breaking syntax?"

7. Alva Noë, *Varieties of Presence* (Cambridge, MA: Harvard University Press, 2012), 147.

8. Pavese, "Skill in Epistemology I," 644. For a neo-Rylean defense of the distinction between knowing how and knowing that, see Ellen Fridland, "Knowing-How: Problems and Considerations," *European Journal of Philosophy* 2, no. 3

(2012): 703–27, and Fridland, "Problems with Intellectualism," *Philosophical Studies* 165, no. 3 (2013): 879–91.

9. Santanu Das, *India, Empire, and First World War Culture: Writings, Images, and Songs* (Cambridge: Cambridge University Press, 2018), 346; subsequent citations are made parenthetically.

10. Sosa, *A Virtue Epistemology*, 22, 23.

11. Sosa's position is a kind of "virtue epistemology" because, like "virtue ethics," the argument prioritizes the condition of the agent herself: "a performance is apt only if its success is sufficiently attributable to the performer's competence." Ibid., 22n1.

12. Noë, *Varieties of Presence*, 2.

13. Michael Strevens, "What Is Empirical Testing?" (2008), http://www.strevens.org/research/episteme/Empirica.pdf.

14. Carl Hempel, *Aspects of Scientific Explanation* (New York: Free Press, 1965), 3.

Chapter Four

1. I take the combination of novelty and value to define the concept of creativity. See Elliot Samuel Paul and Scott Barry Kaufman, "Introducing the Philosophy of Creativity," in *The Philosophy of Creativity: New Essays*, ed. Paul and Kaufman (Oxford: Oxford University Press, 2014), 3–16; and Berys Gault, "Creativity and Skill," in *The Idea of Creativity*, ed. Michael Krausz, Denis Dutton, and Karen Bardsley (Boston: Brill, 2009), 83–103. The value here would be epistemic as well as aesthetic, a kind of truth built into the making.

2. Friedrich Schleiermacher, *Hermeneutics and Criticism and Other Writings*, trans. Andrew Bowie (Cambridge: Cambridge University Press, 1998), 3; subsequent citations are to this edition and are made parenthetically.

3. "*The vocabulary and the history of the era of an author relate as the whole from which his writings must be understood as the part, and the whole must, in turn, be understood from the part....* Complete knowledge is always in this apparent circle, that each particular can only be understood via the general, of which it is a part, and vice versa. And every piece of knowledge is only scientific if it is formed in this way" (24).

4. Hans-Georg Gadamer, *Truth and Method*, trans. Joel Weinsheimer and

Donald G. Marshall (New York: Continuum, 2013), 123; subsequent citations are to this edition and are made parenthetically.

5. On the limits of Gadamer's pluralism, see John Brenkman, "Critical Response I: Response to Jonathan Kramnick, 'Criticism and Truth,'" *Critical Inquiry* 48, no. 1 (2021): 167–71.

6. Sosa, *A Virtue Epistemology*, 29.

7. This is not to say that faculty in English or literature departments only write about writing, as the long history of writing across word and image or word and embodied performance and more recent work across the field of new media would abundantly attest. Nothing in this book is meant to constrain our understanding of what goes on in academic departments. Rather, the point is to consider what, *ceteris paribus*, are the medium conditions for work in the discipline. The art of writing about writing has a core relation to method, practice, and rationale, one distinct, as I'll attempt to show, from other disciplines that work on language.

8. Jas Elsner, "Art History as Ekphrasis," *Association of Art Historians* 33 (2010): 11. See also W. J. T. Mitchell, *Picture Theory* (Chicago: University of Chicago Press, 1994), esp. 83–107.

9. Idan Landau, "Constraining Head-Stranding Ellipsis," *Linguistic Inquiry* 51 (2020): 281. The marks prior to the shading represent the head, the shaded mark the ellipsis.

10. For both linguistics and philosophy of language, the marks form, in the jargon, a *metalanguage* to understand the *object language* under consideration. For my purposes, the important thing to notice is that the creation of a metalanguage at once establishes distance and alters the medium.

11. Guillermo Del Pinal, "Meaning, Modulation, and Context: A Multidimensional Semantics for Truth-Conditional Pragmatics," *Linguistics and Philosophy* 41 (2018): 169. Del Pinal's article was one of the winners of the 2018 *Philosopher's Annual* article of the year prize.

12. Other disciplines work on texts without formalizing their language into an object language of course (intellectual history, political theory), but their arguments typically depend less (or not at all) on aptness of quotation or imitative extension or summary. Their aptness takes a different form.

13. Geoffrey Hartman, *Criticism in the Wilderness: The Study of Literature Today* (1980; New Haven, CT: Yale University Press, 2007), 161; subsequent citations are made parenthetically.

14. George Puttenham calls hendiadys "the figure of Twynnes" and offers

several examples, including "Not you coy dame your lowrs nor your lookes. For [your lowrying looks]" and "Of fortune nor her frowning face.... In stead, of [fortune's frowning face]." George Puttenham, *The Arte of English Poesie* (1589; Birmingham, 1869), 188. On the classical origin and early modern use of the trope, see George T. Wright, "Hendiadys and Hamlet," *PMLA* 96 (March 1981): 168–93.

15. Geoffrey Hartman, *The Unremarkable Wordsworth* (Minneapolis: University of Minnesota Press, 1987), 29.

16. William Wordsworth, "Lines Written a Few Miles above Tintern Abbey," in *The Major Works*, ed. Stephen Gill (New York: Oxford, 2008), 131.

17. The idea of placing "it is true that" in front of a proposition in order to deflate the meaning of truth derives from Gottlob Frege: "It is ... worthy of notice that the sentence 'I smell the scent of violets' has just the same content as the sentence 'it is true that I smell the scent of violets.' So it seems, then, that nothing is added to the thought by my ascribing to it the property of truth." Gottlob Frege, "The Thought: A Logical Inquiry," in *Readings in the Philosophy of Language*, trans. A. M. and Marcelle Quinton, ed. Peter Ludlow (Cambridge, MA: Harvard University Press, 1997), 12. The deflationary theory of truth that descends from Frege is important for my current purposes because it provides the grounds for thinking that once questions of "aptness" have been sorted, no further question of truth lingers.

18. Anne Whitehead, "Writing with Care: Kazuo Ishiguro's *Never Let Me Go*," *Contemporary Literature* 52, no. 1 (2011): 56.

19. The distinction is usually credited to the Russian formalists; see, e.g., Viktor Shklovsky, *The Theory of Prose* (1929), trans. Benjamin Sher (Champaign: University of Illinois Press, 1990), 170.

20. Sharon Marcus, "Reading as If for Death," *Critical Inquiry* 48, no. 3 (2022): 449; subsequent citations are made parenthetically.

21. See Jonathan Kramnick, "What We Hire in Now: English by the Grim Numbers," *Chronicle of Higher Education*, December 9, 2018, https://www.chronicle.com/article/what-we-hire-in-now-english-by-the-grim-numbers/.

22. Ibid.

Chapter Five

1. For a defense of disciplines as epistemic units structured in a nonreductive relation to a variegated world, see my *Paper Minds*, esp. 17–36. The idea is

that "pluralistic array of disciplines matches up with a pluralistic vision of the world" (17).

2. Stanley Fish, *Is There a Text in This Class?: The Authority of Interpretive Communities* (Cambridge, MA: Harvard University Press, 1980), 343; subsequent citations are made parenthetically.

3. See ibid., 11 passim.

4. So, for example, when Fish's near-allies Steven Knapp and Walter Benn Michaels take on the question of knowledge in "Against Theory," they simply assert, contra nearly every canon of epistemology, that "knowledge and true belief are the same." Steven Knapp and Walter Benn Michaels, "Against Theory," *Critical Inquiry* 8, no. 4 (1982): 738. They are "the same," in other words, regardless of whether one is justified in having the beliefs one has (let alone whether, after Gettier, justified true beliefs actually are knowledge). Without any role for justification, Knapp, Michaels, and Fish have no way of accounting for why a belief should count as knowledge and seemingly no interest in coming up with such an account, hence their scorn for method.

5. Stanley Fish, *How Milton Works* (Cambridge, MA: Harvard University Press, 2002), 472, 467; subsequent citations are made parenthetically.

6. On the methodological and philosophical background, see Fiona Fidler and John Wilcox, "Reproducibility of Scientific Results," *Stanford Encyclopedia of Philosophy*, December 3, 2018, plato.stanford.edu/entries/scientific-reproducibility/; and Holm Tetens, "Reproducibility, Objectivity, Invariance," in *Reproducibility: Principles, Problems, Practices, and Prospects*, ed. Harald Atmanspacher and Sabine Maasen (Hoboken, NJ: Wiley, 2016), 13–20.

7. For a recent overview and discussion, see Clare Wilson, "The Replication Crisis Has Spread through Science—Can It Be Fixed?" *New Scientist*, April 6, 2022, https://www.newscientist.com/article/mg25433810-400-the-replication-crisis-has-spread-through-science-can-it-be-fixed/#ixzz7WDb85NzT. See also *Nature*'s lead editorial and survey in issue no. 533, May 26, 2016.

8. Rolf A. Zwaan, Alexander Etz, Richard E. Lucas, and M. Brent Donnellan, "Making Replication Mainstream," *Behavioral and Brain Sciences* 41 (2018): 1–61. This is an especially important formulation because it is from a target article for a special issue on the replication crisis and the foundations of science in one of the nation's leading journals of cognitive science and psychology.

9. See Karl Popper, *Conjectures and Refutations* (London: Routledge, 1963), 43–77.

10. This is a separate, though obviously related, matter from the aesthetic judgment of works of literature and other arts, the note on which John Brenkman's response to the initial version of my argument ends and the subject of spirited vindication in Michael W. Clune's *A Defense of Judgment* (Chicago: University of Chicago Press, 2021). Clune's emphasis on the conditions of expertise is, however, directly relevant to the present discussion (see esp. 65-107), as is John Brenkman's emphasis on persuasion (see "Critical Response I: Response to Jonathan Kramnick," 171).

11. "apt, *adj.*," *OED Online*, Oxford University Press, https://www.oed.com/view/Entry/9969.

12. Immanuel Kant, *Critique of Judgment* (1790), trans. Werner S. Pluhar (Indianapolis: Hackett, 1987), 89; subsequent citations are to this edition and are made parenthetically.

13. Again, suspends them in idea if not in practice. "He must believe that he is justified in requiring a similar liking from everyone because he cannot discover, underlying this liking, any private conditions, on which only he might be dependent, so that he must regard it as based on what he can presuppose in everyone else as well. He cannot discover such private conditions because his liking is not based on any inclination he has (nor on any other considered interest whatever): rather, the judging person feels completely *free* as regards the liking he accords the object." Ibid., 54. See also Anahid Nersessian, "For Love of Beauty: Literary Criticism in Troubled Times," *New Left Review* 133/134 (2022), esp. 192-95.

14. See my *Paper Minds*, 74-97; and Abigail Zitin, *Practical Form: Abstraction, Technique, and Beauty in Eighteenth-Century Aesthetics* (New Haven, CT: Yale University Press, 2020), esp. 54-83.

15. Jonathan Richardson, *An Essay on the Theory of Painting* (London, 1725), 24.

16. David Pye, *The Nature and Art of Workmanship* (London: Cambridge University Press, 1968), 18.

17. For reflections on the structure of peer review in science, its fallibility and need for monitoring, and the ultimately communal character of scientific knowledge, see Helen Longino, *Science as Social Knowledge: Values and Objectivity in Scientific Inquiry* (Princeton, NJ: Princeton University Press, 1990), esp. 68-69.

18. See the lead editorial and survey in *Nature*, no. 533, May 26, 2016.

19. Here I follow Jennifer Lackey's argument that disagreement among experts is only intractable when we consider experts as authorities rather than advisors. Using the latter, we can rely on peer judgment and review and leave room for dis-

agreement. See Jennifer Lackey, "Experts and Peer Disagreement," in *Knowledge, Belief, and God: New Insights in Religious Epistemology*, ed. Matthew Benton, John Hawthorne, and Dani Rabinowitz (Oxford: Oxford University Press, 2018), 228-45.

Coda

1. For a history of the term "public humanities" and a discussion of its varied meanings in the context of academic labor, see Robyn Schroeder, "The Rise of the Public Humanists," in *Doing Public Humanities*, ed. Susan Smulyan (London: Routledge, 2020), 5-27.

2. Judith Butler, "The Future of the Humanities Can Be Found in Its Public Forms," *MLA Newsletter* 54, no. 2 (2020): 2.

3. Carin Berkowitz and Matthew Gibson, "Reframing the Public Humanities: The Tensions, Challenges, and Potentials of a More Expansive Endeavor," *Daedalus* 151, no. 3 (2022): 69-70.

4. Judith Butler, "The Public Futures of the Humanities," *Daedalus* 151, no. 3 (2022): 44.

5. Leonard Cassuto and Robert Weisbuch, *The New PhD: How to Build a Better Graduate Education* (Baltimore: Johns Hopkins University Press, 2021), 317.

6. I stated at the outset that this is not a historical study. Allow me, however, to observe that the desire to make academic knowledge public by means of a changed platform is coincident with the very emergence of criticism in the eighteenth century, articulated memorably by Joseph Addison in *The Spectator*: "It is said of Socrates that he brought philosophy down from Heaven, to inhabit among Men; and I shall be ambitious to have it said of me, that I have brought Philosophy out of Closets and Libraries, Schools and Colleges, to dwell in Clubs and Assemblies, at Tea-Tables, and in Coffee-Houses." Joseph Addison, *Spectator*, no. 10, in *The Spectator*, 5 vols., ed. Donald Bond (Oxford: Oxford University Press, 1965), 1:44. For more on this, see Jonathan Kramnick, *Making the English Canon: Print-Capitalism and the Cultural Past, 1700-1770* (Cambridge: Cambridge University Press, 1999), and "Literary Criticism among the Disciplines," *Eighteenth-Century Studies* 45, no. 3 (2002): 343-60.

7. The use of this kind of first person is an important and innovative feature of some recent academic criticism as well. Among the works cited in this book, see in particular Christina Sharpe's *In the Wake*, including the chapter with the discussion of *Beloved* cited earlier.

8. Margaret Ronda, "Poetry for the Deluge," *Public Books*, February 16, 2022, https://www.publicbooks.org/environmental-poetry-climate-catastrophe/.

9. Elissa Myers, "Charlotte Brontë's OCD," *Los Angeles Review of Books*, June 2, 2021, https://avidly.lareviewofbooks.org/2021/06/02/charlotte-brontes-ocd/.

10. Omari Weekes, "New York Is Now: Colson Whitehead's Civil-Rights-Era Crime Novel," *Bookforum*, September/October/November 2021, https://www.bookforum.com/print/2803/colson-whitehead-s-song-of-civil-rights-era-harlem-24623. The recent demise of *Bookforum* (initially listed in my first paragraph and then stricken when it closed shop) represents the vulnerability of public criticism to market forces less veiled and mediated than those facing academic criticism.

11. "Our Mission," *Public Books*, https://www.publicbooks.org/about/.

12. Gus Stadler as quoted in Katie Kadue, "The End of the Star System," *Chronicle Review*, January 3, 2023, https://www.chronicle.com/article/the-end-of-the-star-system.

13. "Our Mission," *Public Books*.

Index